HOMOSEXUAL DESIRE

Guy Hocquenghem

Translated by Daniella Dangoor

Allison & Busby, London

First published in Great Britain 1978
by Allison and Busby Limited
6a Noel Street, London, W1V 3RB
Reprinted 1978

ISBN 0 85031 206 X
ISBN 0 85031 207 8

Library of Congress Catalog Card Number: 78-000-338

Set in 11/12pt Baskerville and printed by
Billing & Sons Limited, Guildford, London and Worcester

Xmas. 79.

To: Richard .

All my loVG

HOMOSEXUAL DESIRE

Alan

X

CONTENTS

For Gérard Grandmontagne, who committed suicide
in Fresnes prison on 25 September 1972

PREFACE

by Jeffrey Weeks

Guy Hocquenghem's *Homosexual Desire,* first published in France in 1972, represents a juncture between the politics of homosexuality and a number of significant French leftist theoretical and political currents. These currents have, on the whole, been absent from most English-language debates until very recently, and their appearance now can be seen as the outcome of a certain deadlock in traditional English-language thinking about sexual politics. Hocquenghem's essay itself should not be seen as a defintive theoretical statement nor as a clear guide to current practice. Its value lies rather in its summing up of important intellectual tendencies, and their specific application to the question of homosexual oppression.

The focal point of the essay, unifying its theoretical elements and giving it its distinctive élan and vitality, is the possibility of social and personal transformation which was opened up by the May events in France in 1968, and which poses, in Hocquenghem's view, the opportunity for a "revolution of desire". But the specific argument of the essay is guided by the new possibilities for a radical sexual politics opened up by the emergence of the gay liberation movement in the early 1970s. The movement, which began in the United States in 1969 and rapidly spread to Western Europe in 1970-1, stressed the necessity for a new, open, homosexual politics, a *revolutionary* politics (in rhetoric if not in form) which had as its underlying thrust the goal of personal and sexual self-determination. It is the idea of homosexuals taking control of their own identities, and in doing so rejecting the stigmatising labels of a hostile society, which poses a real challenge to bourgeois ideologies of familial and reproductive sexuality and male dominance. Hocquenghem sees this transformation of the politics of homosexuality as itself an expression of the new possibilities signalled in 1968.

9

In outlining this position Hocquenghem identifies with a series of overlapping French intellectual projects, themselves partly transformed by the impact of the theoretical and political stirrings of the late 1960s : the "recovery of Freud" associated with Jacques Lacan; the linguistic theories derived from Ferdinand de Saussure and others; the debate on ideology and the "constitution of the subject" stimulated by the work of Louis Althusser; the anti-psychiatry concepts of Gilles Deleuze and Félix Guattari; the historical discussions around the work of Michel Foucault. There is in these a major concern with language, psychoanalysis and marxism which provides the theoretical framework of *Homosexual Desire*. A major interest of the work is its attempt to describe, using this framework, how the "homosexual" as a social being is constituted in a capitalist society, and the consequences of this for gender and sexual identities. The book itself explores this in three parts : first, it describes and analyses the "paranoid" hostility to homosexuality that modern society reveals; second, it relates this to the role of the Oedipal family and reproductive sexuality in modern capitalism; third, the work states the possibilities of anti-capitalist and anti-Oedipal struggles afforded by the gay movement along with other autonomous movements and "subject groups".

Although there has been a long-standing hostility towards male homosexual behaviour in the Christian West, the modern form of this is of relatively recent origin. As Hocquenghem indicates, it was the late nineteenth century which saw the embryonic emergence of notions which have dominated twentieth-century views : in particular the idea of homosexuality as a disease or sickness (the "medical model") and that homosexuality represents a specific individual "condition", deriving either from a tainted heredity or a corrupting environment. This represented both a secularisation of the old religious sanctions and an individualisation of the condition, and was associated with a general increase of social hostility and an "internalisation" of guilt. Even the reformers, such as Magnus Hirschfeld in Germany or Havelock Ellis in Britain, worked within the framework of homosexuality as a specific individual "variation" or "anomaly". This much was common throughout America and Western Europe.[1] But inevitably, there were major national divergences in social and especially legal responses. Unlike Britain and Germany, France saw no tightening of the law in the late nineteenth or early twentieth centuries, and there was a consequent absence of any major legal scandals such as that of Oscar Wilde in England. Under the Napoleonic legal code, homosexuality as such was not subject to specific legal sanctions until 1942. In that year the collaborationist Pétain régime in nazi-occupied France imposed penalties for homosexual offences with "minors" under the age of twenty-one. Before this, the "age of consent" was sixteen, and was applied to heterosexuality and homosexuality alike. The Pétain enactments were confirmed by the post-liberation régime of General de Gaulle in 1945, and it was under the later Gaullist régime of the 1960s that a further tightening of the law took place, when the penalties for public "indecency" were raised, more sharply for homosexual than for heterosexual offences. Thus while social-democratic régimes in England and Wales, Holland, Germany and Scandinavia were liberalising the law on male homosexuality in 1960s, the authoritarian Gaullist régime was extending it. (But it is worth noting, in passing, that even in "liberal" Britain the reformed law of 1967 was severely limited in its extent, and was followed by an actual increase in police prosecutions relating to "public decency".) This partly explains the specific form of homosexual politics in France. There has in fact been a French homosexual organisation, known as Arcadie, in existence since the mid 1950s, and is now reputed to have over 50,000 members. But this has been notoriously conservative and closeted. A small, short-lived revolutionary homosexual group did appear in the post-1968 surge of energy, but it was not until 1971 that a gay liberation grouping, the *Front Homosexuel d'Action Révolutionnaire* (FHAR) appeared, explicitly modelled on the American Gay Liberation Front. Although small, it was important in politicising the question of homosexuality. *Homosexual Desire* reflects these developments, and its aim is clearly to see homosexual oppression as an inevitable part of a wider system of exploitation and oppression. Hence its echoes of Herbert Marcuse's precepts on the moral "totalitarianism" of modern capitalism and its references to Wilhelm Reich; but more central are the discussions of Freud, the references to the work of Lacan, and the specific criticisms of Lacanian psychoanalysis

11

produced by Gilles Deleuze and Félix Guattari in their joint work *L'Anti-Oedipe: Capitalisme et Schizophrénie*[2]. *Homosexual Desire*, in both its title and its major concepts, demonstrates in particular the author's involvement with the latter work. To understand properly certain formulations used by Hocquenghem, therefore, we must first clarify the terms of the debate.

Desire

The starting-point of this debate is the dialogue with psycho-analysis as theory, technique and practice, and its focus is the return to Freud outlined by Jacques Lacan, a "return" to a Freud purged of the biologism for which he is usually criticised by feminists and focusing on his central discovery, the uncon-scious. For Lacan and his followers, Freud's work represents the beginnings of a new science of the unconscious whose aim is to uncover the truth of the subject, the "individual" as a social being. But, as Althusser has put it,

> "Freud had to think his discoveries and his practice in imported concepts, concepts borrowed from the thermo-dynamic physics then dominant, from the political economy and biology of his time".[3]

In the hands of Freud's followers (who were encouraged, it has to be said, by tendencies in his own writings) psychoanalysis became a system, heavily encased in the irrelevances of other disciplines, and an orthodoxy in which the major insights were overlaid by a sort of psychic determinism. Lacan, helped by the fact that in France, unlike Britain or the United States, psycho-analysis had never been complicit with medical authority, sought to draw out the kernel of Freud's revolutionary discoveries. In this interpretation, as Juliet Mitchell has said:

> "Psychoanalysis is about the material reality of ideas both within, and of, man's history. . . .
>
> The way we live as 'ideas' the necessary laws of human society is not so much conscious as *unconscious* — the particular task of psychoanalysis is to decipher how we acquire our heritage of the ideas and laws of human society within the unconscious mind."[4]

12

The unconscious mind, as she goes on to say, is the way in which we acquire the laws of society, for the unconscious is created as the animal child becomes a human child by entering into the social world through the process and resolution of the Oedipus crisis — the acceptance of the "law of the Father", the fundamental law of society. Through this process, the child enters the symbolic order, an order of signs, meanings, language. Lacan's theorisation would itself have been impossible without the emergence of a new science of linguistics, associated especially with the work of Saussure. For Lacan, "the discourse of the unconscious is structured like a language", and it is through language that the child enters the adult (social) world. Thus Lacan's return to Freud involved a particular emphasis on certain of his works, such as *The Interpretation of Dreams,* where Freud studied the mechanisms and laws of dreams, reducing the variants to two, displacement and condensation. For Lacan, following linguistics, these become metonomy and metaphor. The return, in other words, is to a Freud whose concern is with the unconscious processes of symbolic transformations.[5]

What Lacan set out to do was recover the subversiveness of Freud: the key element which has made Lacan influential both among anti-psychiatrists and on the left is the rejection of the coherence of the "ego" or "self", of an essential "individual". For a marxist such as Louis Althusser, for example, Lacan's work opened the way to an understanding of the "structure of misrecognition", or the forms in which the human subject conceives the world; this has been of particular concern therefore to some recent theorists of ideology.[6] The project, here, is the fit between the insights of psychoanalysis as a theoretical tool and marxism. Marx recognised that the individual human subject is not the "centre" of history, as bourgeois thought believed, and that history has no given centre except in ideological misrepresentation. And this articulates with Freud's discovery, as conceived in Lacanian psychoanalysis, that the individual subject has no given centre or consciousness, but is "de-centred", dominated by a law which he does not create but which creates him. Lacan undermines those ideas of the "self" as a coherent whole which are implicit in our language and ideologies.

But as well as suggesting an entrée for marxist theories of

13

ideology, Lacan's interpretation of psychoanalysis is a major link with the anti-psychiatry movement which, in France as in Britain (where it has been represented by the writings of R. D. Laing and David Cooper), has stressed the continuity between madness and reason, so that the decentred self is not qualitatively distant from the fragmentation of the schizophrenic experience. This is a theme developed and transformed by Deleuze and Guattari. It is relevant here because an important part of the radicalism of the late 1960s laid stress precisely on the marginal, the mad, the criminal, as rejectors of bourgeois society, as standing outside the dominant forms of authority and order, the Lacanian "symbolic order".

But a third element needs stressing, for Lacan's recovery of Freud has also been suggested as a basis for understanding patriarchy and the structures of male dominance. It is a key to grasping the ways in which the animal child enters the social world as a boy or a girl, the unconscious ways in which psychological "masculinity" and "femininity", and male dominance, are accepted as necessary parts of becoming social beings. Such an understanding is essential for a feminist politics. A sketch of Lacan's theory will clarify this process, and also partly explain some of the terms used by Hocquenghem.

The human infant is seen as being concerned at first with the exploration of sensory perceptions, and its main characteristic is its autoerotism. It has no sense of its physical separateness, nor of its physical unity. This is the moment which retrospectively is referred to as the phantasy of the "body in pieces". The *mirror-stage* is the moment when the infant realises the distinction between its own body and the outside, the "other". It is expressed metaphorically in terms of the child seeing itself in the mirror and identifying with its reflection. But the image is ever external to the child, so that this mirror-stage announces the permanent alienation at the heart of identification. The process of identification inaugurates the *imaginary* relation, where the individual misrecognises himself as the perfect image which appears in the mirror and with which the individual identifies, as being everything he imagines himself to be. As interpreted by Althusser this becomes a key term in the understanding of ideology, as an "imaginary" (but not "false") misrecognition of the world.

14

Following the mirror-stage, the first form of identification with an object outside the infant is with the mother, a relationship which determines the attitude of the child to the zones of its own body, according to the significance given to them within the relationship. The fact that the genital aspect of the infant's relationship to the mother cannot be developed brings this pre-Oedipal phase to an end. The Oedipus complex is the stage when the intervention of the Father necessitates the child's abandonment of its exclusive relationship with the mother and its entry into the structures of human sexuality. The child is assigned a position in language and the family, in structures of "masculinity" or "femininity". The repression of those elements of the psychic life of the child which do not conform to this positioning constitutes the unconscious.

It is in the unconscious that the child carries the very structures of a patriarchal society. The child's attempt to include genital functions amongst those expressive of the identification of mother and child are unsuccessful because the child has a rival in the Father, against whom it is powerless. This is not necessarily a real male parent but rather the symbolic representation of all Fathers : the Father is the authority which dominates the mother-child relation. Confronted with this authority the child now sees the mother, formerly the repository of all identity, as a testimony only to the authority of the Father. The opening of this fundamental "absence" in identity inspires the fear of castration, in both boy and girl, though the specific forms vary. This is what forces the resolution of the Oedipal crisis, when the child enters the social world, which Lacan calls the Symbolic, the order of language; the child identifies with certain terms — boy, girl, son, daughter — which receive their significance as ideas through their relation to a central "signifier" (in Lacan's usage a cluster of words, images, ideas) the *Phallus,* the symbolic expression and representative of the authority of the Father. This is intimately connected with the notion of *desire*; indeed, as Juliet Mitchell has put it, the phallus is the very mark of human desire. It is the expression of a fundamental absence which can never be fulfilled, the desire to be the other, the Father, which is both alienated and insatiable : alienated because the child can only express its desire by means of language which itself constitutes

15

its submission to the Father; and insatiable because it is desire for a symbolic position which is itself arbiter of the possibilities for the expression of desire. The Phallus and Desire are thus key elements, and represent and express the individual's submission to the laws of society. Just as "desire" cannot be equated with organic or biological need, so the "phallus" is not coterminous with the physical penis: it is the representation, the signifier of the laws of the social order, the law of the Father, through which obedience to the social (and patriarchal) order is instilled.

What Lacan is attempting to theorise is not a biological development but a social process, and what he is describing are not so much actual events (for example, the threat of castration) as symbolic acts. Thus, as Juliet Mitchell has said, "In 'penis envy' we are not talking about an anatomical organ, but about the ideas of it that people hold and live by within the general culture", and this can be applied to other phases. Hence the analogies, in Lacan as in Freud, with drama, the theatre. As Althusser has put it,

> "The Oedipus complex is the dramatic structure, the 'theatrical machine' imposed by the Law of Culture on every, involuntary, conscripted candidate to humanity."[8]

What Lacan is describing is the human drama whereby each animal child becomes part of the social world, expressing its structures as a social being.

Against Oedipus

The major problem is that Lacan, like Freud, appears to make these stages, and the Oedipus complex, a transhistorical human experience, though for Lacan it is essentially a cultural not a biological experience. Even Juliet Mitchell, who believes the Law of the Father can be eventually overcome, believes it to be a necessary element in patriarchal societies.

For Deleuze and Guattari, as for Lacan, the forms of desire are not set in nature but are socially created. But they reject psychoanalysis, and in doing so construct a challenge to Oedipus as a *necessary* stage in human development. They attack Lacan for staying *within* the Freudian family framework: as a result,

16

psychoanalysis is trapped within capitalist economic and social demands. Their challenge is expressed in their book *L'Anti-Oedipe : Capitalisme et Schizophrénie*, which was first published in French in 1972. Gilles Deleuze is a philosopher and writer on literature while Félix Guattari was trained as a Lacanian psycho-analyst and has been a marxist activist. Their book, which claimed to re-energise the debate on the relationship between Freud and Marx, created a considerable stir on publication in France and led them to be compared with Laing and Cooper as enemies of psychiatric orthodoxies. Like Lacan, whose writing is complex and unconventional (Freud's readability is often criti-cised for leading to oversimplification), Deleuze and Guattari attempt to challenge conventional language as well as conven-tional theory, with the result that in *L'Anti-Oedipe* we are presented with a picture of a world whose complexity and flux defy language. This expresses their basic objection to Freudian theories : any concept of Oedipus implies artificial restrictions on a field, the unconscious, where everything is in fact infinitely open. Deleuze and Guattari see man as constituted by "desiring machines". Infinite types and varieties of relationships are possible; each person's machine parts can plug into and unplug from machine parts of another. There is, in other words, no given "self", only the cacophony of desiring machines. Fragmen-tation is universal, and is not the peculiar fate of what society defines as the schizophrenic. But the crucial point is that capitalist society cannot live with the infinite variety of potential intercon-nections and relationships, and imposes constraints regulating which ones are to be allowed, i.e. essentially those relating to reproduction in the family. Psychoanalysis, by accepting the familial framework, is trapped *within* capitalist concepts of sexuality, concepts which distort the production of desire. Psycho-analytic theory, by concentrating on the Oedipal triangulation of parents and child, reflects the social, political and religious forms of domination in modern society, and is complicit with how capitalism has constructed the family. Deleuze and Guattari argue that the individual's consciousness is not determined by a closed family system, but by a historical situation. So they can analyse and criticise the family, for example, in terms of the desires expressed during May 1968. Desire then becomes an

17

element in the social field, an active participant in social life, not just an element in the individual's psyche. The Oedipus complex, instead of being, as in Lacan, a necessary stage in the development of the human individual, is seen by Deleuze and Guattari as the only effective means of controlling the libido in *capitalist* society. So Freudianism plays a key role under capitalism: it is both the discoverer of the mechanisms of desire, and the organiser, through its acceptance of the Oedipus complex, of its control. For at a time when capitalist individualisation is undermining the family by depriving it of essential social functions, the Oedipus complex represents the internalisation of the family institutions, it is a policeman of the mind.

Deleuze and Guattari develop their analysis of the relationship between the Oedipalised family and the needs of capitalist society through their theory of entropy (increasing disorder), using concepts borrowed from French anthropological debate. Desiring machines can be coded or decoded: coding puts information about the society and its social language into place, decoding decreases social information. Decoding represents an increase in entropy and it results in society losing control of the machine's interconnections, or "flux". Schizophrenia represents the boundary of decoding. Deleuze and Guattari suggest that as society becomes more "civilised" (capitalist), the level of code in the desiring machines decreases; society struggles against the progressive loss of shared meaning as it would be destroyed by total decoding (schizophrenia). The family is therefore constructed as an artificially "re-territorialised" unit where social control has been relocated and in which forms of social organisation can be reproduced. The father becomes a familial despot, and the mother, for example, an image for earth and country. Thus the privatised "individual" that psychoanalysis studies within the Oedipal family unit is an artificial construct, whose social function is to trap and control the disorder that haunts social life under capitalism.

Thus psychoanalysis can neither understand desire nor suggest an alternative. As their alternative, Deleuze and Guattari suggest what they term "schizoanalysis", a process of decoding whose aim is to uncover the unconscious activities of desire in the social field, and the role of the family in responding to the social need

18

to avoid disorder. Where psychoanalysis understands social events in terms of the family, schizoanalysis approaches the family in terms of social needs. And the goal is an emergent understanding of desire. In modern society we can become "neurotic", that is, accept our Oedipalisation (and use psychoanalysis); or we can reject it, by becoming what society describes as "schizophrenic"; or we can adopt a third alternative, and "schizophrenise" — that is, we can reject the false coherence of the "molar" self, and this will lead us to an experience of the self at the "molecular" level of our desiring machines. We can set out to discover the desiring machine, a process which Deleuze and Guattari, echoing Laing, call a "voyage" of discovery, and in doing so the "truth of the subject" will become clearer.

Such a precept has clear political implications, which feed into Hocquenghem's work. For the aim is to find unalienated forms of radical social action, and these cannot be traditional centralised structures (especially of the working class), because these, too, are complicit with capitalism. The model of alternative modes was provided by the spontaneous forms of activity developed in France in 1968, "fusions of desire" which escape the imprisoning force of the "normal". Schizoanalysis provides the alternative: the schizophrenic is not revolutionary, but the schizophrenic process is the potential of revolution, and only in the activity of autonomous, spontaneous groupings, outside the social order, can revolution be achieved. The result, which is central to Hocquenghem's project, is a worship of the excluded and marginal as the real material of social transformation.

The most fierce polemics against these concepts have come from other French marxists. Thus Henri Lefebvre has written,

"It takes a good deal of philosophical arrogance to state, as Deleuze and Guattari do in *L'Anti-Oedipe,* that capitalism only prolongs itself by generating a flux of inanities. . . . It is simply the hypothesis of Bergsonian philosophy revised and corrected by psychoanalysis. By separating time from space, it turns the schizoid into an explanatory principle. It is the belated theorisation of a version of 'leftism' that has run aground on the politicisation of this or that real but peripheral issue (prison, drugs, insanity, etc.) and has then sunk back into a negation of the political. Unfortunately,

19

this also means that they have handed the situation back to the 'pure' politicians."[9]

There is much force in this diatribe, especially in pinpointing the failure to confront the ultimate question of power in society. For instance, can one regard all the "marginals" as being of equal specific weight? But before discussing some of the problems we must look at the influence of these ideas on Hocquenghem.

The Sublimated Anus

Hocquenghem employs the theoretical concepts discussed above, firstly to locate hostile attitudes to homosexuality within a theory of family and reproductive sexuality, and secondly to provide the outline of a politics which can challenge and overthrow these attitudes. His project is explicitly a revolutionary one and in delineating it Hocquenghem skilfully synthesises a wide range of debates.

Of particular relevance to an understanding of homosexuality is his recognition of the social and culturally specific function of the definition of "the homosexual". Very few cultures, in fact, have had a developed concept of the "homosexual" as a specific type of person different from the "normal" or "heterosexual" person and in the West it was essentially a creation of the nineteenth century. Moreover, in terms of self-identification on the part of those so defined, it is still an emergent and not an achieved identity. We may note here the influence of the work of the historian, Michel Foucault. Hocquenghem makes explicit references to Foucault's essay on *Madness and Civilization,* which traces the growth in the eighteenth century of the social concept of madness as a specific individual quality. Hocquenghem makes the point that what he calls the "growing imperialism" of society seeks to attribute a social status and definition to everything, even the unclassifiable, and the result has been that homosexuality, traditionally conceived of as a possibility in all sinful creatures (otherwise, why the often severe religious sanctions?), has from the nineteenth century been seen as a specific characteristic (often a "disease") of a particular ("sick" or "degenerate") type of individual. Foucault's most

20

recent work, *La volonté de savoir*, makes this point explicitly.[10] It seems to me an essential starting-point for any discussion of homosexuality to recognise this fundamental point, for otherwise we lose ourselves (as most essays into "homosexual history" do) in a welter of arguments over whether a particular individual was homosexual or not. The core of the problem is (a) what is the effect on individual lives of social definitions of "the homosexual" (or by analogy the "mad", "schizophrenic", etc.), and (b) what are the conditions for the emergence of such definitions and individual meanings.

Hocquenghem confronts these questions by challenging the notion of "homosexual desire", which he sees as itself misleading. "Desire", properly speaking, is neither homosexual nor heterosexual. Desire, as Deleuze and Guattari state, is "emergent", and its components are only discernible *a posteriori*. Homosexual desire, like heterosexual desire, is an arbitrary division of the flux of desire, an "arbitrarily frozen frame" in an unbroken and polyvocal flux. The notion of exclusive homosexuality is therefore a "fallacy of the imaginary", a misrecognition and ideological misperception. But despite this, homosexuality has a vivid social presence and Hocquenghem asks — and answers — why. The answer is that homosexuality expresses an aspect of desire which is fundamentally polymorphous and undefined, which appears nowhere else, and that it is more than just sexual activity between members of the same sex. For the direct manifestation of homosexual desire opposes the relations of roles and identities necessarily imposed by the Oedipus complex in order to ensure the reproduction of society. So homosexuality is artificially trapped within the grid of "civilisation" and created as an abstract, separate, and excoriated division of desire.

Capitalism, in its necessary employment of Oedipalisation, manufactures "homosexuals" just as it produces proletarians, and what is manufactured is a psychologically repressive category. Homosexuality is artificially cut off from desire, and placed in a separate category. He therefore suggests that the principal ideological means of thinking about homosexuality, which date back to the turn of the century, are intimately, though not mechanically, connected with the advance of Western capitalism. They amount to a perverse re-territorialisation, a massive effort to

21

regain social control in a world tending towards disorder and decoding. Moreover, the establishment of homosexuality as a separate category goes hand in hand with its repression. The result on the one hand is the creation of a scapegoated minority of "homosexuals", and on the other the transformation of the repressed homosexual elements of desire into the desire to repress : hence sublimated homosexuality is the basis of the paranoia about homosexuality which pervades social behaviour, and of the panic that the mere mention of the word creates.

It is here that the anti-psychiatry emphasis of Deleuze and Guattari becomes relevant, for Hocquenghem sees that psychiatry has played a vital part in the installation of guilt (expressed, as he notes, even in the works of homosexual writers such as Proust). So the psychiatrisation of homosexuality has not superseded penal repression, it has accompanied it. For if repression is to be effective, the culprit must recognise it as necessary, so that modern repression demands an interplay between legal guilt and the psychology of guilt; this is achieved precisely by the Oedipal moment, the victory of the Law of the Father, which is vital for the fulfilment of institutional laws.

Though cogently argued, a number of doubts must arise, not so much about the descriptive elements (which empirical work on attitudes to homosexuality tend to validate) as about the theoretical argument. Three specific questions need to be more fully confronted. Firstly, there is the whole question of homosexual "paranoia". There can be no doubt that many non-homosexuals display a hysterical hostility towards homosexuality; in recent Anglo-Saxon writings this has been defined as "homophobia".[11] But the idea that repression of homosexuals in modern society is a product of repressed homosexuality comes too close to the hydraulic theory of sexuality (the notion that there is a fixed amount of energy which sublimation re-distributes) which the Lacanian recovery of Freud sought to undermine. It is not a sufficient explanatory principle simply to reverse the idea peddled by the medical profession that homosexuality is a paranoia into the idea that attitudes to homosexuality are merely paranoid. It does not, for instance, explain the real, if limited, liberalisation of attitudes that has taken place in some Western countries, nor the range of attitudes that are empirically known to exist in different

22

countries and even in different families. Hocquenghem suggests that the relaxation of legal penalties is in effect itself a new form of repression (in Marcusean terms this could be called "repressive desublimation"), but this does not itself provide a basis for grasping the *shift* in the location of social taboos (for example, in Britain in the 1970s from adult male homosexuality to paedophilia).

Secondly, there is the problem of why some individuals become "homosexual" and others (the majority?) do not. Hocquenghem's theories usefully suggest the artificial (and social) nature of the division between "homosexual" and "heterosexual", but do not fully explain the processes involved, except in terms of the general Oedipal processes. How, for instance, does the individual enter the symbolic order as a "homosexual" rather than a "heterosexual"? What are the specific family pressures, the educational processes, the media images that reinforce the identity? The key reference-point is "reproduction", both of the species and of the Oedipal relationships, as Hocquenghem indicates, but this poses important historical and theoretical problems that demand further exploration.

A third difficulty is closely related to this: Hocquenghem's failure to explore the different modalities of lesbianism. It is important to note that what Hocquenghem is discussing is essentially male homosexuality, for in Hocquenghem's view, although the Law of the Father dominates both the male and the female, it is to the authority of the Father in reproduction (both of the species and of Oedipalisation itself) that homosexuality poses the major challenge; as Deleuze and Guattari note, male homosexuality, far from being a product of the Oedipus complex, as some Freudians imply, itself constitutes a totally different mode of social relationships, no longer vertical, but horizontal. Lesbianism, by implication, assumes its significance as a challenge to the secondary position accorded to female sexuality in capitalist society. It is not so much lesbianism as female sexuality which society denies. But Hocquenghem quite fails to pursue this point, which is central if we are to grasp the formation of sexual meanings. It is a criticism which has been cogently levelled at the Lacanian school of psychoanalysis that at the same time as helping us to understand the "phallocentric" view of sexuality, it

23

actually surrenders to it. In a patriarchal society, female sexuality is defined in relationship to the male. The paradox remains theoretically unexplained (and not only in this work) as to why lesbianism, which ultimately asserts the automony of female sexuality, has historically been ignored, by the absence of legal oppression and even in the work of early liberal sexologists such as Havelock Ellis. Lesbianism has a different history from male homosexuality, and poses specific problems (for example, why did a specific lesbian identity emerge later than a male homosexual identity?), but Hocquenghem's work lacks completeness in failing even to pose the question.

This failure relates to the core of Hocquenghem's theory, which is summed up in the sub-section entitled "The Phallic Signifier and the Sublimated Anus" (p. 81). Hocquenghem argues that only one organ is allowed in the Oedipal triangle, that which Deleuze and Guattari call the "despotic signifier", the Phallus. And as money is the fetish, the true universal reference-point for capitalism, so the Phallus is the reference-point for heterosexism. Ours is a phallic (or "phallocratic") society. The Phallus determines — whether by absence or presence — the girl's penis envy, the boy's castration anxiety; it draws on libidinal energy in the same way as money draws on labour. And our society is phallic to such a degree that the sexual act without ejaculation is seen as a failure. The result is a denial of all other forms of sexuality, and in particular, the anal. And here is the key to the argument. For while the Phallus is essentially social, the anus is essentially private; and for the organisation of society around the great phallic signifier to be possible, the anus must be privatised. Hocquenghem quotes Deleuze and Guattari, to the effect that the anus was the first organ to be privatised, and Freud, who sees the anal stage as the stage of the formation the self. The result is that the "anus is over-invested individually because its investment is withdrawn socially".

Homosexuality, Hocquenghem argues, chiefly means anal homosexuality, sodomy. It is always connected with the anus, even though, as all the empirical evidence (such as Kinsey's) suggests, anal intercourse is still the exception even among homosexuals. In our patriarchal society, only the Phallus is a dispenser of identity, and any social use of the anus other than a subli-

24

mated one creates the risk of a loss of identity, whether the individual is a man or a woman. Hocquenghem quotes Freud's remark that "the anal becomes the symbol of all that must be dismissed from [the individual's] life". The conclusion is that homosexual desire is the operation of a desiring machine "plugged into the anus".

Clearly, what Hocquenghem is suggesting cannot have a literal meaning (as he says, the empirical evidence does not bear this out); the intention is to suggest the symbolic consequence of the dominance of the Phallus. He uses it to argue that since the anus has been privatised by capitalist/phallic domination, we need to "group" it, which means, in effect, to reject the individualised notion of homosexuality as a problem. Practising homosexuals are those who have failed their sublimation, who therefore can and must conceive their relationships in different ways. So when homosexuals as a group publicly reject their labels, they are in fact rejecting Oedipus, rejecting the artificial entrapment of desire, rejecting sexuality focused on the Phallus. And they are rejecting the Symbolic Order. But the major problem here is that the emphasis on the anal has clearly a metaphorical rather than a properly scientific meaning. The historical facts seem to be that the emphasis on sodomy decreased as the conceptualisation of "the homosexual" increased. In Britain for instance, sodomy carried the death penalty until 1861, but it was *after* the reduction of this penalty (to between ten years and life) that the real process of social definition, and an increase in social hostility, began.

There is an obvious danger in challenging theoretical concepts with historical data, and Hocquenghem is correct to stress the peculiar horror of sodomy that still survives. But without a fuller explanation it is all too easy to believe that the core of Hocquenghem's theory is a flawed attempt to fit his explanatory theses into given Freudian categories. His theory does, however, have the useful function of challenging the centrality of reproductive sexuality : the anal may be seen as a metaphor for this, and it leads to some suggestive insights. He argues that when the anus recovers its desiring function (i.e. when the Phallus loses its centrality), when laws and rules disappear, group pleasures will appear without the "sacred difference" between public and

25

private, social and individual. And Hocquenghem sees signs of this "sexual communism" in institutions of the gay subculture, where "scattering" or promiscuity, representing polymorphous sexuality in action, reigns. This point is rarely made and is valuable, challenging as it does the usual condemnation of promiscuity. It can, of course, be overstated. The problem remains for gay people of working out life-styles and forms of relationship which break away from heterosexist norms; these cannot necessarily be derived from styles that have developed as a reaction to social oppression. For Hocquenghem, however, there is an important political point to be made. He suggests that the "cruise" (the search for sexual partners) of the homosexual male is reminiscent of what *L'Anti-Oedipe* describes as the "voyage" of the schizophrenic. Hocquenghem suggests that a promiscuity freed from guilt is the very mode of desire itself. Homosexuals, therefore, breaking free of their guilt, are like the schizophrenics in Deleuze and Guattari's work, the models of revolutionary potential.

Hocquenghem, then, rejects both the traditional homophile movements, with their timidity and acceptance of the artificial divisions of desire, and the traditional leftist organisations. He seeks to show how the struggles of homosexuals have challenged the accepted relationship between desire and politics. Hocquenghem suggests, like Deleuze and Guattari, that there is no real revolutionary centre; the "centre" lies on the fringes, the marginal. He suggests that we should question the whole basis of "civilisation", understood as the Oedipal succession of generations, and that we should fight, with Fourier (and also, though Hocquenghem does not mention him, with the early English socialist Edward Carpenter) against "civilisation", "the interpretative grid through which desire becomes cohesive energy", which bolsters the capitalist order. So, like Deleuze and Guattari, Hocquenghem looks to the spontaneous and non-organised workers' movements, ecological movements, community politics and the "politics of experience", and the gay movement, as the material for radical transformation. Autonomous movements which refuse the law of the Signifier, and are brought into being by particular desiring situations, reject traditional political logic and completely upset the political world.

26

Hocquenghem is here expressing simultaneously the euphoric optimism of post-1968 radicalism and the despair of the traditional politics of the working class, which in the 1960s could be read into the work of Herbert Marcuse and others. Hocquenghem's political outlook rightly stresses the vitality and significance of the new, autonomous movements; more than "protest" movements, they are attempts at real self-determination. Of course, they are not all of equal social significance, but their very appearance, and their impact on a generation of young radicals, was a significant index of the appalling absences in traditional left attitudes. It is noticeable, certainly in Britain, that the traditional groups of the revolutionary left have had to take real notice of many of the new groupings, especially of the women's movement, which had hitherto all too readily been rejected as "petty bourgeois". However, Hocquenghem's emphasis on the centrality of "subject groups", through which desire is introduced into the social sphere, ignores the complex articulation of the various movements, with each other and with the working-class movement. In rejecting the myth of the "normal" as natural and given, and in emphasising the need for conscious struggle against it, Hocquenghem, like Deleuze and Guattari, is in danger of creating a new myth: the revolutionary potential of the marginal, a myth which ignores the real problems of power, physical and ideological, in modern capitalism. Hocquenghem poses here a challenge to traditional concepts of social transformation, without finally responding to it.

The personal and the political

The concerns of French radical debate have had their parallels in Britain and North America — in the former largely because of the failures of social democracy, in America largely under the impact of the Vietnam War and the crisis of American imperialism. In fact, the major autonomous movements that Hocquenghem cites — the women's, black and gay movements — all appeared in North America first. But though the concerns have been similar, the intellectual traditions through which they have been expressed have discrete origins.

We have already noted the common anti-psychiatry trends in

27

the work of Deleuze and Guattari on the one hand, and Laing and Cooper on the other, and their specific concern with schizophrenia. Juliet Mitchell has usefully summed up the relevance of this in England :

> "Laing's early analyses of schizophrenia as a disturbance induced by immediate interaction within the family helped to introduce a new phase of radical humanism to which the women's movement is heir. Both within Laing's own thought and within the theses of those it reflected and inspired, the plight of the scapegoated driven-mad was generalisable. Western society dehumanised persons, categorising them into oppositional stereotypes of mad/sane, black/white and so on. The radical counter-ideology of the restoration of 'whole' (i.e. 'individual') people was thus introduced."[12]

Thus while French anti-psychiatry had clear antecedents in psychoanalysis, the British rejected this tradition from the start and derived many of their concepts from existentialist thought, and had a more clearly individualised outlook. The result was the predominant "personalism" of the British radicalism of the late 1960s and early 1970s, leading to a pervasive form of radical humanism. This became vitally important in the emergence of the "new politics" in Britain and America, and led to efforts to sustain a "radical psychology", as well as influencing the sexual liberation movements. It is worth noting that the first functional group set up in the London Gay Liberation Front was a counter-psychiatry group.

This radical humanism was also clearly reflected in tendencies in sociology in Britain which provided the theoretical basis for the activities of the "new politics". An important element of this was summed up in the so-called "radical deviancy" school of sociology, the chief expression of which was the National Deviancy Conference, set up in 1968 by a number of criminologists who rejected the traditional institutional and Home Office approach to crime.[13] The chief feature of this was the realisation that deviance and crime are not inherent qualities of "actors" but are social definitions that become attached to individuals in a process of social interaction with other people. This had important theoretical implications, which were expressed

28

in an essay by Mary McIntosh, "The Homosexual Role", exploring how concepts of a specific homosexual "condition" and a defensive subculture emerged in the eighteenth and nineteenth centuries in England.[14] We should remark here that notions of the social nature of definitions of homosexuality (or any other social "deviancy") were emerging at roughly the same period in both France and Britain, but through different theoretical routes. In Britain, too, there was a noticeable tendency to glorify the role of the outsider, in radical politics. The theoretical framework here, however, was clearly not marxist at this stage, and there was no engagement as yet with psychoanalysis.

The dominant theoretical framework in Britain derived from "symbolic interactionism", ultimately an outgrowth of structural functionalism and the sociology of knowledge. Here ideas are not treated in terms of their historical roots or practical effectiveness, but are seen as forming the background to every social process. Social processes are treated essentially in terms of ideas, and it is through ideas that we construct social reality itself. Most of the most valuable work that has informed the theoretical study of homosexuality in Britain has derived from symbolic interactionism (e.g. Kenneth Plummer's Sexual Stigma, which is the major British study of how homosexual meanings are acquired).[15] In this theory sexual meanings are constructed in social interaction: a homosexual identity is not inherent, but is socially created. This has had a vitally important clarifying influence, and has, for instance, broken with lay ideas of sex as a goal-directed instinct. But symbolic interactionism has been unable to theorise the sexual variations that it can so ably describe; nor can it conceptualise the relations between possible sexual patterns and other social variables. It is unable to theorise (and it is here that Hocquenghem's ideas are relevant) why, despite the endless possibilities of sexualisation it suggests, the genitals continue to be the focus of sexual imagination, nor why there are, at various times, shifts in the location of the sexual taboos. And there is a political consequence too, for if meanings are entirely ascribed in social interaction, an act of collective will can transform them: this leads, as Mary McIntosh has suggested, to a politics of "collective voluntarism". Both in theory and practice it ignores the historical location of sexual taboos. Symbolic interactionism,

29

in other words, stops short at precisely the point where the French debate begins — at the point of social determination and ideological structuring in the creation of subjectivity.

It is precisely for this reason that a number of British feminists have begun to explore the work of Lacan and others, with a view to developing a theoretical understanding of patriarchy. The focal point has been Juliet Mitchell's *Psychoanalysis and Feminism* which, as a sympathetic critic recently stated,

> "Opens the way to a re-evaluation of psychoanalysis as a theory which can provide scientific knowledge of the way in which patriarchal ideology is maintained through the foundation of psychological 'masculinity' and 'femininity'. Such knowledge is obviously a precondition of any successful cultural and political struggle against patriarchy — the point being not merely to understand the unconscious but to change it."[16]

This approach points to the need for specific ideological practices in combating patriarchy, although the ways in which this might be done are so far scarcely in outline. It presents, too, the necessity for the struggle of autonomous groupings as an aspect of the struggle against capitalism and for socialism. But there is a twofold problem. First, what form should these specific struggles take? And secondly, what is the relationship between these autonomous groupings and the wider struggle, especially that of the working class, for socialism? It is a pertinent criticism of Mitchell that she completely separates the various struggles in such a way as to reproduce the economism for which marxists are usually criticised by feminists. She seems to see the working class (guided by marxism) as fighting for socialism at the economic and political level, while the women's movement (guided by psychoanalysis) is fighting against patriarchy at the ideological level. In other words, instead of applying historical materialism to the understanding of subjectivity, she effectively sees two separate sciences for two separate objects of study.

Mitchell's book has, however, been of great significance in stimulating the necessary discussions in the women's movement and the gay movement. And partly as a consequence of its appearance, recent developments in Britain and elsewhere suggest a new interest in the French theoretical debates. In 1977 Lacan's *Ecrits* appeared for the first time in an English translation, while a number of journals have explicitly confronted the relevance of the theoretical debates (for example, *Ideology and Consciousness,* which began to appear in London in 1977). The evolution of one Australian journal sums up the theoretical trajectory: founded as the *Gay Liberation Fress* in 1972 in Sydney, it later became *GLP: A Journal of Sexual Politics,* and finally in 1976 emerged as *Working Papers in Sex, Science and Culture,* with the aim of critically examining "the function of language, ideology and scientificity in the construction of sex theories ranging from conventional sciences to liberation movements." The first two issues made the journal's concerns explicit by particularly examining the work of Lacan, Althusser and Juliet Mitchell.

It is in this developing context that Hocquenghem's book becomes relevant, for it touches on a major controversy in the whole debate about Lacan and patriarchy: the transhistoricity of the dominance of the Phallus. Lacan has been criticised of late by feminists for the phallocentric nature of his work. Hocquenghem, as we have seen, following Deleuze and Guattari, gives the dominance of the Phallic a specific (if undefined) historical location. This should provide a valuable focus for further debate, for his endeavour is clearly to link "sexual oppression" to the forms of capitalism, thus posing the need for a common struggle (*pace* Juliet Mitchell) against patriarchy and against capitalism. No work so far has clearly theorised these links, and further debate around this question is vital. There are acute dangers, of course, in Hocquenghem's schema. As Lefebvre's polemic (quoted above) suggests, the need still remains on the left for a clarification of the nature of the necessary combination between socialist political struggle and the various social movements that are, in their different ways, fighting bourgeois norms.

Hocquenghem's essay is born of a specific conjuncture of theoretical and political concerns, and cannot, of course, attempt to confront all the outstanding issues. But the questions he raises, both implicitly and explicitly, are important now: the relationship of sexual identity to patriarchal structures; the fit between patriarchy and capitalism; the forms of struggle necessary to

31

combat both. A critical reading of Hocquenghem's essay must help in re-opening the necessary debate on these issues.

NOTES TO PREFACE

1. See Jeffrey Weeks, *Coming Out! Homosexual Politics in Britain from the Nineteenth Century to the Present*, London, Quartet, 1977, chapters 1-3.
2. Gilles Deleuze and Félix Guattari, *L'Anti-Oedipe: Capitalisme et Schizophrénie*, Paris, Les Editions de Minuit, 1972.
3. "Freud and Lacan", in Louis Althusser, *Lenin and Philosophy*, London, New Left Books, 1971, p. 182.
4. Juliet Mitchell, *Psychoanalysis and Feminism*, London, Allen Lane, 1974, p. xvi.
5. For an interpretation of Freud heavily influenced by Lacan, see Octave Mannoni, *Freud: The Theory of the Unconscious*, London, New Left Books, 1971.
6. See Louis Althusser, *op. cit.;* "On Ideology", in *Working Papers on Cultural Studies*, Birmingham (1977 edition); *Ideology and Consciousness* No. 1, May 1977; *Papers on Patriarchy*, Women's Publishing Collective, Lewes, 1977.
7. Juliet Mitchell, *op. cit.*, p. xvi.
8. Louis Althusser, *Lenin and Philosophy*, p. 198.
9. Henri Lefebvre, *The Survival of Capitalism*, London, Allison and Busby, 1976, p. 34.
10. Michel Foucault, *Histoire de la sexualité* vol. 1: *La volonté de savoir*, Paris, Gallimard, 1976. An introduction to the ideas contained in this work can be found in Colin Gordon, "Birth of the Subject", in *Radical Philosophy*, no. 17, Summer 1977.
11. For a discussion of this concept see George Weinberg, *Society and the Healthy Homosexual*, New York, St Martin's Press, 1972. For a critique see Ken Plummer, "The Homosexual Taboo", in *Gay News* no. 106, London, 1976.
12. Juliet Mitchell, *op. cit.*, p. xviii.
13. For a discussion of this see Mary McIntosh, "Modern Trends in Sociology", in *Marxism Today*, September 1977.
14. Mary McIntosh, "The Homosexual Role", in *Social Problems*, vol. 16, no. 2, Autumn 1968.
15. Kenneth Plummer, *Sexual Stigma: An Interactionist Account*, London, Routledge and Kegan Paul, 1975.
16. Randall Albury, "Two Readings of Freud", in *Working Papers in Sex, Science and Culture*, vol. 1, no. 1, January 1976, p. 7.

1
INTRODUCTION

The problem is not so much homosexual desire as the fear of homosexuality: why does the mere mention of the word trigger off reactions of recoil and hate? We shall therefore be investigating the phantasies and ratiocinations of the heterosexual world on the subject of "homosexuality". The great majority of "homosexuals" are not even conscious of being such. Homosexual desire is socially eliminated from childhood by means of a series of family and educational mechanisms. The power of oblivion generated by the social mechanisms with respect to the homosexual drive is such as to arouse the immediate answer: this problem does not concern me.

We shall start with what is commonly known as "male homosexuality". This does not mean that the difference in the sexes goes without saying; on the contrary, it must in the end be questioned. But the organisation of desire to which we submit is based on male domination, and the term "homosexuality" refers first and foremost to the imaginary Oedipal construction of male homosexuality. It would be futile to keep trying to deal with the subject of female homosexuality in terms of male ideology.

There are drives of desire which all of us have felt and which nevertheless do not affect our daily conscious existence. That is why we cannot come to terms with what we believe about our own desire. There is a social mechanism forever wiping out the constantly renewed traces of our buried desires. One simply has to think about what happens with an experience as widespread as masturbation to realise how powerful this mechanism is: everybody has masturbated, yet no one ever mentions it, not even to their closest friends.

"Homosexual desire" — the expression is meaningless. There is no subdivision of desire into homosexuality and heterosexuality. Properly speaking, desire is no more homosexual than

35

heterosexual. Desire emerges in a multiple form, whose components are only divisible *a posteriori,* according to how we manipulate it. Just like heterosexual desire, homosexual desire is an arbitrarily frozen frame in an unbroken and polyvocal flux. The exclusively homosexual characterisation of desire in its present form is a fallacy of the imaginary; but homosexuality has a specially manifest imagery, and it is possible to undertake a deconstruction of such images. If the homosexual image contains a complex knot of dread and desire, if the homosexual phantasy is more obscene than any other and at the same time more exciting, if it is impossible to appear anywhere as a self-confessed homosexual without upsetting families, causing children to be dragged out of the way and arousing mixed feelings of horror and desire, then the reason must be that for us twentieth-century westerners there is a close connection between desire and homosexuality. Homosexuality expresses something — some aspect of desire — which appears nowhere else, and that something is not merely the accomplishment of the sexual act with a person of the same sex.

Homosexuality haunts the "normal world". Even Adler could not refrain from acknowledging the fact:

> "The problem of homosexuality hovers over society like a ghost or a scarecrow. In spite of all the condemnation, the number of perverts seems to be on the increase. . . . Neither the harshest penalties nor the most conciliatory attitudes and most lenient sentences have any effect on the development of this abnormality."[1]

In its endless struggle against homosexuality, society finds again and again that condemnation seems to breed the very curse it claims to be getting rid of.

And for a very good reason. Capitalist society manufactures homosexuals just as it produces proletarians, constantly defining its own limits: homosexuality is a manufactured product of the normal world. This statement must not be taken in the liberal sense as acquitting the homosexual of his offence and assigning the guilt to society, a falsely progressive position which turns out to be even more ruthless towards homosexuals than open repression. Nobody will ever eliminate the polyvocality

36

of desire. But what is manufactured is a psychologically repressive category, "homosexuality" : an abstract division of desire which allows even those who escape to be dominated, inscribing within the law what is outside the law. The category under discussion, as well as the term indicating it, is a fairly recent invention. The growing imperialism of a society seeking to attribute a social status to everything, even to the unclassifiable, has created this particularisation of the imbalance : up to the end of the eighteenth century, people who denied the existence of God, could not speak or practised sodomy were locked up together in the same prisons. The advent of psychiatry and mental hospitals manifests society's ability to invent specific means for classifying the unclassifiable (see Foucault's *Histoire de la Folie à l'âge classique*); this is how modern thought has created a new disease, homosexuality. According to Havelock Ellis,[2] the word "homosexual" was invented in 1869 by a German doctor. Dividing in order to rule, psychiatry's modern pseudo-scientific thought has turned barbarous intolerance into civilised intolerance.

Psychiatry has thus classified what is marginal, but in doing so has placed it in a central position. Kinsey's prodigious adventure is a lesson to us. He merely continued modern psychiatry's efforts to encompass everything by providing it with material, sociological and statistical foundations; in a world dominated by numbers, he demonstrated that homosexuals may be relegated to a mere 4 or 5 per cent. And it was certainly not these few millions who were responsible for the storm which broke out on the publication of the Kinsey report, but a discovery which no amount of scientific naïveté could hide :

> "Since only 50 per cent of the population is exclusively heterosexual throughout its adult life, and since only 4 per cent of the population is actively homosexual throughout its life, it appears that nearly half (46 per cent) of the population engages in both heterosexual and homosexual activities, or reacts to persons of both sexes, in the course of their adult lives."[3]

It is no longer a matter of the little "queer" everybody knows, but of one person out of two — your neighbour, maybe even your own son. And Kinsey naïvely writes on :

"The world is not to be divided into sheep and goats. Not all things are black nor all things white. It is a fundamental of taxonomy that nature rarely deals with discrete categories. Only the human mind invents categories and tries to force facts into separated pigeon-holes. The living world is a continuum in each and every one of its aspects."[4]

By constantly discriminating and "discerning", we fall into the indiscernible. Was it really necessary to send out so many questionnaires and investigations in order to establish that everyone is more or less homosexual? The rights of quantitative normality were later to be restored by the famous Kinsey scale, which indexes individuals according to their degree of homosexual practice, reducing the percentage level to the amount of homosexual instinct present in each person.

Thus the margins close in on the norms of sexuality and gnaw at them persistently. Every effort to isolate, explain, reduce the contaminated homosexual simply helps to place him at the centre of waking dreams. Sartre is basically right here, whatever other criticisms are to be made of his psychological portrait of Genêt: why does society always call on the psychiatrist to speak and never on the homosexual, except in the sad litany of clinical "cases"?

"What matters to us is that he does not let us hear the voice of the guilty man himself, that sensual, disturbing voice which seduces the young men, that breathless voice which murmurs with pleasure, that vulgar voice which describes a night of love. The homosexual must remain an object, a flower, an insect, a dweller of ancient Sodom or the planet Uranus, an automaton that hops about in the limelight, anything you like except my fellow man, except my image, except myself. For a choice must be made: if every man is all of man, this black sheep must only be a pebble or must be me."[5]

Difference may breed security, but the mere word "pederast"* turns out to be strangely seductive: "pederasque" (as in

---

* The French word *pédéraste* is used in everyday speech as a synonym for "homosexual" (*trans.*).

"tarasque", the medieval dragon of Provençal legends), "pederastre" (as in "Zoroastre"). These common slips of the French tongue appear in letters to newspapers, and are enough to convey what happens at the mere utterance of the word. The exceptional richness of the vocabulary indicating the male homosexual deserves at least to be mentioned : queer, fag, fairy, queen (using the masculine or feminine gender arbitrarily), etc., as if language were exhausting itself in trying to define, to name the unnamable.

And if we constantly need to repeat that there is no difference between homosexuals and heterosexuals, that both are divisible into rich and poor, male and female, good and bad, then this is precisely because there is a distance, because there is a repeatedly unsuccessful effort to draw homosexuality back into normality, an unsurmountable chasm which keeps opening up. Homosexuality exists and does not exist, at one and the same time : indeed, its very mode of existence questions again and again the certainty of existence.

2
ANTI-HOMOSEXUAL PARANOIA

The establishment of homosexuality as a separate category goes
hand in hand with its repression. It is therefore no surprise to
find that anti-homosexual repression is itself an indirect manifestation of homosexual desire. The attitude of what is commonly called "society" is, in this respect, paranoiac: it suffers
from an interpretative delusion which leads it to discover all
around it the signs of a homosexual conspiracy that prevents
it from functioning properly. Even Martin Hoffman, an honest
sociologist with no imagination, acknowledged in his book *The
Gay World* that such a paranoia exists. A film like *Hunting
Scenes from Bavaria* gives a good account of the consequences
of the paranoiac interpretative delusions of a Bavarian village
towards the person on whom the entire population's homosexual libido is focused: in the hunt sequence which ends the
film, the representative of that desire is cut off from all ties with
the community. The appearance of a recognisable or avowed
homosexual directly results in an unreasoning panic terror of
being raped among those around him. The tension in the confrontation between a homosexual and an individual who considers himself normal is created by the instinctive question in
the mind of the "normal" individual: Does he desire me? As if
the homosexual never chose his object and any male were good
enough for him. There is a spontaneous sexualisation of all
relationships with a homosexual.

Psychiatry generally acknowledges a close relation between
homosexuality and paranoia, but more often than not attributes
to it a form in which the homosexual frequently suffers from
a persecutory paranoia: he "feels threatened". This is one of
the main clinical characteristics of the "homosexual". Homosexuality falls within the sphere of medicine, and the words
of the homosexual are of interest or value only if they are
filtered through the psychiatric screen. This is an inversion of

41

perspective, attributing to the individual the paranoiac discourse which in fact arises from the situation. Does the homosexual only feel threatened, or is he really threatened? Society's discourse on homosexuality (which is internalised by the homosexual himself) is the fruit of the paranoia through which a dominant sexual mode, the family's reproductive heterosexuality, manifests its anxiety at the suppressed but constantly recurring sexual modes. The discourse of medical men, judges, journalists and educators is a permanent effort to repress the homosexual libido.

Freud's famous "persecutory paranoia" is in actual fact a paranoia that *seeks to persecute*. The reversal of meaning which Freud's concept has undergone in this respect is enlightening. Freud states that persecutory paranoia is generally connected with the repression of the libido's homosexual component. Social man's fear of his own homosexuality induces in him a paranoiac fear of seeing it appear around him. Freud analyses the Schreber case (1911) in the following terms:

> "We should be inclined to say that what was characteristically paranoiac about the illness was the fact that the patient, as a means of warding off a homosexual wishful phantasy, reacted precisely with delusions of persecution of this kind. These considerations therefore lend an added weight to the circumstance that we are in point of fact driven by experience to attribute to homosexual wishful phantasies an intimate (perhaps an invariable) relation to this particular form of disease."[6]

And furthermore:

> "We were astonished to find that in all these cases a defence against a homosexual wish* was clearly recognisable at the very centre of the conflict which underlay the disease, and that it was an attempt to master an uncon-

---

* The German *Wunsch* is translated as "désir" in the French standard edition of Freud and as "wish" in the English. All quotations from Freud here are taken from the English standard edition, but in the rest of the text, "désir" is translated by its English cognate "desire". For an explanation of the difficulties of translation and the Lacanian concept of desire, see Laplanche and Pontalis, *The Language of Psychoanalysis*.

sciously reinforced current of homosexuality that they had all of them come to grief."[7]

It is the inevitable failure of the attempt to remove the homosexual component that is the origin of the paranoia. The assumption appeared scandalous enough to Freud himself to warrant an apology to society as a whole:

"Is it not an act of irresponsible levity, an indiscretion and a calumny, to charge a man of such high ethical standing as the former Senatspräsident Schreber with homosexuality?"[8]

Freud knew the hornets' nest he was stirring up:

"I will pause here for a moment to meet a storm of remonstrances and objections. Anyone acquainted with the present state of psychiatry must be prepared to face trouble."[9]

And if we extricate ourselves from the Oedipal framework to which Freud instantly confines his invention, we can see that Freud's essential discovery is not Schreber's relationship with his father but the fact that a man with as clearly specified a social position as a judge's can, but must not, be homosexual. Imagine a trial in which Schreber-the-judge had to settle some common incident such as the corruption of a minor or indecent exposure. The Schreber case is the limit to which a society is prepared to go: we can find no other instance of a high official publicly voicing his homosexual phantasies (Schreber allowed his book *Memoirs of my Nervous Illness* to be published in his own lifetime) without ending up in a mental hospital. Senatspräsident Schreber was allowed to continue enjoying his wealth and his office. The Schreber case testifies to the strength of a society which can afford, in exceptional moments, to see through the reality of its administrators' psyche. Schreber is a conscious paranoiac, for he himself expresses the content of his phantasies with the utmost clarity.

Freud shares the discovery of the connection between homosexuality and paranoia with Ferenczi. In an article dated 1911, "On the Part Played by Homosexuality in the Pathogenesis of Paranoia", Ferenczi notes that the resort to paranoia is the

43

conversion of the feeling of love into the perception of its opposite : "interest becomes persecution". And he specifies :

"It has become evident . . . that *the paranoiac mechanism is not set in action as a defence against all possible attachments of the 'sexual hunger', but, according to the observations made up to the present, is directed only against the homosexual choice of object* [italics in original]. . . . In the pathogenesis of paranoia, homosexuality plays not a chance part, but the most important one, and . . . paranoia is perhaps nothing else at all than disguised homosexuality."[10]

Paranoia only manifests itself in connection with homosexuality : such a statement challenges heterosexuality's status as the sole normal sexual relationship. The third case which Ferenczi analyses in his article concerns a local government employee (yet another individual in public life, but a minor one incapable of seeing through his own phantasies). This man was in the habit of writing letters to report the fact that an officer who lived opposite him "shaved himself at the window, partly in his shirt, with a bare chest". He kept mentioning the officer's underpants as part of the scandal. We cannot fail to recognise in Ferenczi's description the mechanisms of justice itself, when it purports to be examining a case that concerns public morals :

"It made me suspicious to begin with that he handed me a mass of newspaper cuttings, documents and pamphlets, numbered and sorted in the most exemplary order, all of which he had writtten himself. A glance at the papers convinced me that he was a paranoiac with delusions of persecution."[11]

The patient even owned a press on which he printed his accusations. Yet the honest Ferenczi never voiced any like suspicions about the legal anti-homosexual machinery, whose workings were being reproduced on a smaller scale by the patient. He does, however, interpret the delusion "as projection [of the patient's] own homosexual delight in those persons, the affect being preceded by a negative sign. His desires, which have been cast out from the ego, return to his consciousness as the perception of the persecutory tendency on the part of the objects that unconsciously please him."[12]

The author goes on to say:

> "He seeks until he has convinced himself that he is hated. He can now indulge his own homosexuality in the form of hate, and at the same time hide from himself."[13]

In his merciless struggle against military debauchery, the patient accuses the military authorities of believing him to be "an old woman . . . seeking for the objects of her curiosity". Schreber also took himself for a woman, but not necessarily an old or unattractive one. His paranoia did not have to be fuelled by making feeble accusations because, being the chairman of a court, he had all the available means to construct his own machinery of desire and repression.

Freud and Ferenczi make the point constantly:

> "Insufficiently repressed homosexuality can later, under certain circumstances, become once more manifest. . . . This is especially the case with paranoia . . . [which] is really to be conceived as a disguised manifestation of the inclination towards the person's own sex."[14]

The fate of both society and psychiatry hinges on the "insufficiently" repressed, and therefore the libido's homosexual component is generally only put to social use in a sublimated state:

> "Only a minor part of this component gets rescued in a sublimated form in the cultivated life of adults, in playing, in readiness for social help, in friendship leagues, in club life, etc., a part that is not to be underestimated."[15]

For Freud, too, the emergence of Schreber's homosexuality in the form of paranoia is due to some fault in the repressive social machinery:

> "[Such] people are exposed to the danger that some unusually intense wave of libido, finding no other outlet, may lead to a sexualisation of their social instincts and so undo the sublimations which they had achieved in the course of their development."[16]

There is no use of the homosexual libido other than that which is sublimated for the sake of the social body:

> "Homosexual tendencies are not . . . done away with or brought to a stop; they are merely deflected from their sexual aim and applied to fresh uses. They now . . . help to constitute the social instincts, thus contributing an erotic factor to friendship and comradeship, to *esprit de corps* and to the love of mankind in general."[17]

The analysis of the Schreber case shows the paranoiac attempting "to defend himself against the sexualisation of (his) social instinctual cathexes". Freud takes up the theme again in an article dated 1922, "Some Neurotic Mechanisms in Jealousy, Paranoia and Homosexuality", which concludes as follows:

> "In the light of psychoanalysis we are accustomed to regard social feeling as a sublimation of homosexual attitudes towards objects."[18]

So it is society as a whole that defends itself against the sexualisation of its investments (for example, a homosexual judge), and struggles with all its might against homosexual desublimation. André Morali-Daninos bluntly stated this notion in a popular work of general educational interest (*Sociologie des relations sexuelles*):

> "Were homosexuality to receive, even in theory, a show of approval, were it allowed to break away even partially from the framework of pathology, we would soon arrive at the abolition of the heterosexual couple and of the family, which are the foundations of the Western society in which we live."

Homosexuality must remain within the sphere of nosology, pathology, the neurotic mechanism, pathogenesis, etc.: no name is too terrifying to define it all, as these categories well indicate. In spite of Freud's assertion in *Three Essays on the Theory of Sexuality* that neuroses are equivalent to the negative of perversions, psychiatry as a whole replies: homosexuals are neurotics and paranoiacs. Stekel, in his *Auto-Erotism*, had already reversed the terms of this relation. In 1965, during the

Stockholm conference on homosexuality, W. H. Gillespie reverted to Rosenfeld's assertions on the relation between homosexuality and paranoia, describing homosexuality as "one of the most frequent defence mechanisms used against paranoid anxiety".

He went on to say:

> "Similarly, Thorner stresses the persecutory anxiety in the aetiology of male homosexuality: the patient externalises his internal persecutors and projects his anxiety on to them in the role of a sexual partner."[19]

We reach a point where paranoia becomes the cause of homosexuality, reversing Freud's schema in the crassest possible way. In 1966 Marcel Eck's book *Sodome* appeared, in which he reverts to the medicalisation and psychiatrisation of homosexuality. Freud's discovery has not made much progress in psychiatry: it seems on the contrary that the more we go on, the further we stray from what he brought to light. A Schreber would today cause a bigger explosion than in Freud's time. Society, and its medical manifestation, is suffering from a persecutory delusion. The homosexuality which it represses and sublimates keeps springing from every pore of the social body. It delves all the more violently into the private lives of individuals, although it knows that what goes on there exposes society itself and slips out of reach of the law-courts. It builds more and more repressive barriers, but this proves to be so ineffectual that it feels inextricably bound to the desire which it persecutes.

"Unnatural acts": nature and the law

A court of law is a highly homosexual libidinal site: see the description of the trial of the eponymous hero in Genêt's novel, *Our Lady of the Flowers*. Between the police and the legal system on the one hand and homosexuality on the other, there is an inverted relation of desire which we have already observed in the Schreber case and in one of the cases analysed by Ferenczi. Psychiatry is fond of thinking that the homosexual seeks condemnation, and sees this as a sign of his masochism.

47

In doing so, it evidently tries to account for the desiring relation by ascribing it to the homosexual's psychological persona.

It is significant that ever since the last war (but not before!) the French penal code has referred to homosexuality, and homosexuality alone, as a "crime against nature". This is a case of paranoiac regression: it is a well-known fact that the individualised and rationalised law inherited from the bourgeois revolution and the empire ceased to be based on theological concepts such as "nature". If the code retreats into obscurantism here it is because, when faced with homosexuality, it requires the backing of a universal authority on heterosexual normality. "Acts against nature with a person of the same sex": there's no doubt about it, it is the homosexual act as such which is unnatural. Some of us are part of Nature, and some not. "We feel bound to point out that homosexuality is an aberration, as are all the sexual tendencies . . . which . . . deviate from the normal course of biological sexuality as such," wrote Father Marc Oraison, at a time when the church had not yet undertaken to modernise its doctrines on sexual matters.

It is surprising to see modern legislation reverting to the terms of condemnation cast on homosexuality by St Paul in "Epistle to the Romans" — "men forsaking the natural use of women". Nature here plays its paranoiac role as the supreme segregating authority. The term "unnatural", used by the police in the nineteenth century to describe homosexuals, finds its true definition: it describes the person who is against nature as the guarantor both of desire and of its repression. When Gide in *Corydon* attempts to construct a homosexuality which is biologically based, by means of a comparison with other species, he is simply walking foolishly into the trap, which consists of a need to base the form of desire on nature.

A myth: the progress of public morals

There is a deeply rooted myth in contemporary society, the myth of a consant progress, in terms of bourgeois ideology, towards the liberalisation of public morals and respect for the individual. As a result we frequently hear the contradictory remark, "It's unnatural, but no one's stopping you". This is an imperative

48

belief for a society which proclaims its own perfectibility and the absurdity of any idea of breaking with or challenging it.

Popular ideology on the repression of homosexuality subsists on three myths which conceal the paranoiac conduct of justice.

(1) "No one's stopping you". We generally believe that there is simply no legal repression of homosexuality, that the private life of each individual is his own responsibility. But legal repression exists, and on a vast scale. For instance, the following figures were issued by the Paris prefecture of police for the first *quarter* of 1972 : "With regard to homosexuals, 492 were apprehended in the Bois de Boulogne and 18 in the Bois de Vincennes. . . . The inspection of 39 public bars enabled us to apprehend 49 transvestites." No one should ignore the fact that homosexual clubs in Paris are subjected, in many cases several time a week, to police raids on various pretexts. The judiciary convicted 331 persons for unnatural acts in 1964 and 424 in 1966, and these figures have been increasing since then. These statistics were issued by the Department of Justice, which groups all convictions for homosexuality under one heading.

(2) Another deep-rooted popular belief is that homosexuality, and therefore its repression, is peculiar to the upper classes, and is a part of bourgeois decadence. In fact, out of 1,200 convictions in the three years 1964-66, the Department of Justice statistics referred to more than 300 workers (semi-skilled and skilled), 160 unskilled workers and 80 lower-grade office workers. It is obvious that the Department will convict workers more easily than intellectuals or members of the executive class, but there is evidence that real, growing, full-scale legal repression is being directed at the oppressed classes with regard to homosexuality.

(3) "There are simply a few barbaric remnants in the penal code. We live today in a more tolerant society". We have already noted that the term "unnatural" only appeared in our legal code after the second world war. Far from being more liberal, the French penal code has intensified its repression of homosexuality over the last twenty years. Of course, in several European nations — Germany, Holland, Great Britain and the Scandinavian countries — there has been a reduction in the severity of the laws against homosexuality. But this trend has

49

not been followed in other countries (and particularly not in France). We cannot speak of a general tendency to liberalise the law : in fact there has been a movement in the opposite direction, with the exception of those countries where a specific and temporary political situation — the advent of social democratic parties to power — has led to a mitigation of the law.

In France, homosexuality was not a criminal offence until Pétain. The first law in which the term appeared is an ordinance from Marshal Pétain dated 6 August 1942 : "Whosoever will . . . to satisfy his own passions, have committed one or more indecent or unnatural acts with a minor of his own sex, under the age of twenty-one, will be sentenced to a term of imprisonment from six months to three years and a fine." It is scarcely surprising that the French state ("work, family, motherland") should have introduced such changes : until then, the law on the corruption of minors had been the same whether for homosexual or heterosexual purposes, condemning sexual acts committed with minors under the age of sixteen or, in the case of a complaint being lodged by the parents, eighteen. The new specification was directed against homosexuality as such. Rather more surprising is the fact that, after the war, the penal code contained an article which repeated the exact wording of Pétain's ordinance : the Decree of 8 February 1945 (article 331) sentenced "to a term of imprisonment from six months to three years . . . whosoever will have committed an indecent or unnatural act with a person of the same sex, under the age of twenty-one." What might well be called the "Pétain-de Gaulle law" was passed at the time of the Liberation, a time of liberalisation, hope and progress, as the result of a motion introduced by a Christian Democrat deputy.

There is decidedly a deep desiring relation between the Gaullist régime and homosexuality : the second law on homosexuality, the one concerning indecent exposure, was voted through after de Gaulle's return to power in 1960. Previously the penal code did not discriminate between homosexual or heterosexual indecent exposure. Article 330, paragraph 2, dated 25 November 1960, specifies : "When the indecent exposure consists of an unnatural act with an individual of the same sex, the penalty will be a term of imprisonment from six months to

50

three years and a fine of 1,000 to 15,000 francs." Heterosexual indecency is cheaper: a 500 to 4,500 francs fine only.

The paranoiac nature of the law broke into a debate in the National Assembly at that same period; as a result of a motion proposed by Paul Mirguet on 18 July 1960, an amendment was passed introducing homosexuality into the legislation on social diseases, alongside tuberculosis and alcoholism. Mirguet declared in the course of the debate:

"At a time when our civilisation is dangerously under-populated, and therefore vulnerable, in a world in full development, we must oppose everything that may diminish its prestige. In this field, as in all others, France must set the pace. That is why I ask you to pass my amendment . . . because the laws dealing with prostitution do not exactly touch upon homosexuality, and the government must take up a definite position in order to alert public opinion."

The righteous indignation of Mayor Royer of Tours, who in 1971 lodged a complaint against Jean-Paul Sartre for being the editor of a paper guilty of vindicating homosexuality, had the same ring to it. Persecutory delusion wreaks havoc.

Finally, it is the height of paranoia to prosecute two minors of between eighteen and twenty-one for practising homosexuality and to put the case under the same heading as reciprocal assault and battery. It is the height of paranoia that in cases concerning minors, indirect proof or the examining magistrate's personal conviction is sufficient (there is no need for a complaint to be lodged by the family); that in cases of indecent exposure, action may be taken against someone who does not repel an indecent caress quickly enough; that one simply needs to stay too long in a street urinal to be convicted of indecent exposure; that policemen may go as far as incitement (in Turkish baths, for instance) in order to provoke the offence. Repression does not merely take delight in poking into people's underpants, it seeks the outrage, it provokes it in order to condemn it (such police behaviour is frequent in the USA).

In Belgium it was only in 1965 that a specific bill on homosexuality was passed which, on the pretext of protecting the

51

young, repressed indecent behaviour committed without violence on a minor of the same sex under eighteen years of age. A police captain named Tilmant writing in the *Revue de la gendarmerie belge,* the Belgian police journal, said : "For the purposes of adequate prevention and firm repression, the police force must endeavour to have a thorough knowledge of that secret world (the homosexual world) where, we understand, witnesses are rare and informants reticent."[20] It is clear that on the pretext of protecting young people and the public, the judiciary and the police are pursuing their own libidinal aims. He went on to say : "In the case of homosexuality more than in any other, the old adage 'the police are only as good as their files' takes on its full meaning." I wonder what Ferenczi would have made of this.

The law is clearly a system of desire, in which provocation and voyeurism have their own place : the phantasy of the cop is not some creation of the homosexual's deranged mind, but the reality of a deviant desiring operation on the part of police and judiciary.

The strengthening of anti-homosexual paranoia

Anti-homosexual paranoia is becoming stronger, or at least tending to do so. We cannot accept the liberal attitude : of course these laws exist, but they are a delayed reflection of society's position, they represent an old-fashioned ideology; let's forget about them, or let's change them. Public morals are in fact intricately connected with the law : the increase in convictions for homosexuality is related to an increase in homosexual practice. However, this is the result not of a conscious liberalisation but, on the contrary, of the crisis which is shaking this society in the form of a confrontation between its unconscious forces and its rationalised expression. We are not yet into fascism, but Marcuse has rightly pointed to the increasingly totalitarian nature of the ideology of modern capitalist society. The crisis of the family has led an increasing number of young people to opt out of the parent-child framework. However, this crisis also corresponds to an intensification of fascistic anti-youth tendencies on the part of parents and adults; this has been illustrated by surveys of attitudes towards young people, and by the rise in a new type of criminal activity — the murder of young people by adults, particularly bar-owners. If in 1923 Havelock Ellis, in his final version of his book *Sexual Inversion*, could still argue about whether or not castration is an effective cure for homosexuality[21], no doubt many of our contemporaries are not so very far from the point of contemplating a return to such measures, urged on by the paranoia of the popular press and television over the crimes of "sex maniacs". In April 1972 a medical congress was held in San Remo, Italy, in order to discuss cures for homosexuality such as conditioned reflexes, electric shock therapy, drugs and even surgical operations. A German doctor from Frankfurt, Dr Fritz Douglas Roeder, who gained a great deal of support from the press, has a method of curing homosexuality which involves an operation on the hypothalamus. The repressive mechanism of desire is so effective that homosexuals agree to submit to this kind of treatment, and even ask for it.

Homosexuality and crime

Homosexuality is first of all a criminal category. Certainly, as we shall see later, psychiatry tends to replace legal repression with the internalisation of guilt. But the passage of anti-homosexual repression from the penal to the psychological stage has never actually brought about the disappearance of the penal aspect. Quite the contrary. The penal criminal aspect of homosexuality is neither an accident nor is it simply something to be regretted. In fact homosexuality is a matter of delinquency first and foremost; even if we have to demand the abolition of the laws that strike at homosexuality, we must not see the situation as a temporary or modifiable one but as a necessity and perhaps as an opportunity for homosexual liberation.

Musil's marvellous novel *Young Törless* is a projection of all the phantasies of homosexuality on to the microcosmic society represented by a German public school. The student Basini is subjected and surrenders to homosexual games with Reiting and Beineberg because of a crime: he has stolen money from another student's locker. If he is a thief, he may as well be a

53

"queer". We find the same kind of association in all Genêt's works.

Vautrin's homosexuality in Balzac's *Splendeur et misère des courtesanes* is based on the same link. The reverse side of the love affair between Vautrin and Rubempré is, in Balzac's eyes, that part of the prison which the director points out with disgust to visitors as the section where prisoners of the "third sex" are locked up. And when the magistrate finally succeeds in grasping that the enigmatic Abbé Herrera is in fact the criminal Vautrin, it is because he has identified the priest's relationship with Lucien as a homosexual one: " 'He claimed he was your father.' 'Him, my father?' " and Lucien bursts into tears. Back in his old surroundings, Vautrin meets up again with a former lover who is about to be executed. This libidinal assimilation of the homosexual into the criminal has no connection with any rational concept of law or individual responsibility. The above-mentioned Belgian police captain writes in the same article:

> "A careful surveillance of this particular environment gives us the opportunity to make a very useful documentation for detecting the future male prostitute, murderer and blackmailer."

Of course, homosexuals are in this instance more likely to be the victims than the offenders. But by then it doesn't really matter. Every homosexual is a potential killer. Gustave Macé, the chief of the Paris Sureté at the beginning of the third republic, wrote:

> "There is but one step from blackmail to crime, particularly since the sodomite is always hidden. . . . All sodomites are intelligent, but their minds turn to evil."[22]

No humour intended. The Spanish law on social diseases runs as follows:

> "Clause I, paragraph (i). The following categories of persons are declared to be social dangers: (1) vagrants, (2) pimps, (3) homosexuals . . . (7) the mentally sick who, for want of medical attention, constitute a peril to society . . . (9) drug peddlers . . . (11) those who unite in gangs and whose intent is clearly criminal."

Psychiatry provides arguments in support of this association; in Wilhelm Stekel's *Impotence and the Male,* there is one chapter which is headed "Homosexuality and Criminality." In it he describes the relation between impotence and homosexuality, having already associated impotence with crimes of sexual mania. One patient states, "During orgasm, I become very wild. I must control myself at the height of passion and hold my hands to my sides in order not to injure my partner."[23] The purpose of the psychiatrist then becomes evident : with the more honest patients, "the doctor's task is to help them improve, in order to overcome the unconscious killer in them".

Lautréamont's *Maldoror* contains a most beautifully paranoiac description of the homosexual killer : taking advantage of the child's trust, Maldoror digs his nails into the child's breast.[24] The paranoiac association of homosexuality with crime is not only a defence against the homosexual libido, it also decorates it with blood. A case which recently hit the headlines in France, the case of the "mad killers of Les Yvelines", had a good deal of homosexual libido about it : the two young murderers who, for pleasure only, and without stealing, wantonly killed several people during the summer of 1971, were very closely connected with a homosexual circle in which they had been nicknamed "the killers". In May 1972, the son of one of the victims killed one of the murderers in turn, during the course of a police reconstruction of the crime. Murder calls for murder. But the press, while deploring this return to the law of retaliation, found all sorts of justifications for the second crime, which avenged a father's death. Homosexual murder is paranoiacally experienced as murder for pleasure, the main danger to civilised society. The avenging murder deserves respect because it affirms the rights of the family.

Homosexuality and disease

Homosexuality is not just a delinquent category, it is a pathological one. In the psychiatric sense, of course, but also in a more physical sense : drugs and homosexuality are generally mentioned together in official reports because they seem to hold similar positions in the process of degeneration.

55

Venereal diseases seem to play the leading role in the paranoiac ideology concerning homosexuality. The anti-homosexual measures of 1960 were legitimised by a press campaign which dragged out the old bogey of a resurgence of syphilis. In *Le Monde*[25] M. Chenot, the then Minister of Health, stated about venereal diseases :

> "In fact, the causes may be divided into two categories: the increasing immunity of viruses to antibiotics and the considerable development of homosexuality in every country. . . . How can we fight this recrudescence? By increasing the penalties in force against homosexuals."

A Dr Touraine, a member of the Academy of Medicine, wrote in the *Revue du Praticien* ("The Practitioner's Journal") :

> "It is particularly with syphilis that the rôle of homosexuality is revealed, and the figures given as to its frequency testify to the recent rapid and widespread extension of this role."[26]

We already know about the function of the fear of syphilis in middle-class sexuality as a whole, and to what extent the fear of venereal disease acts as a barrier to sexual normality. The weakening of the free social cover against venereal disease which was more readily available in the past than today, is known to the whole medical establishment. The shame that accompanies the disease, the repressive system by which the social worker has virtual police rights in cases of syphilis (including access to the files and his ability to force the patient to declare all sexual contacts who could have been infected) are sufficient to explain the spread of the disease. It is difficult for someone to admit that he has syphilis. Syphilis is not just a virus but an ideology too; it forms a phantasy whole, like the plague and its symptoms as Antonin Artaud analysed them. The basis of syphilis is the phantasy fear of contamination, of a secret parallel advance both by the virus and by the libido's unconscious forces; the homosexual transmits syphilis as he transmits homosexuality. (The same thing happens in fascist ideology: the healthy confront the degenerate, in a battle on which the fate of our civilisation hangs.)

56

To attempt to make homosexuality respectable by means of psychology is hopeless. When D. J. West[27] advocates "prevention through tolerance", he is crusading for the impossible, for it is difficult to see any point in tolerating something you have already decided to prevent. Any investigation of the causes is in this respect merely an *a posteriori* justification of social repression : this is clear in the case of Havelock Ellis, who concludes his otherwise comprehensive work on homosexuality with the statement that the assertion of homosexuality cannot be tolerated, even if we must tolerate its existence. Hans Giese[28] writes : "Deficiency occurs within order, perversion is against order". For Giese, the deficiency is the loss of reproductive sexuality; the perversion is the assertion of homosexuality.

The French Communist Party has often played the role of a kind of bourgeois superego : it stands for the moral principles which it accuses the ruling class of respecting in theory, only to betray them in fact. It has supported the law of family heterosexuality, in particular by repeatedly adopting a firm stand against abortion. The appearance of a leftist homosexual movement has given it the opportunity to expound the principles of bourgeois morality on this subject. M. Juquin, a member of the central committee, declared in May 1972 : "We must not confuse drugs, sexual perversion or theft with revolutionary action." He also stated, in an interview in *Le nouvel observateur,* that "The cover of homosexuality or drugs has never had anything to do with the workers' movement. . . . There can be no true order unless it is within and by way of democracy."

It is not homosexual behaviour as such at which the moralising paranoia is directed : the fact that one man makes love with another is never the point of this kind of statement. Homosexuality seems rather to represent the detritus of a well-oiled social machine whose workings the Communist Party would like to improve on still further; it is what remains of the unclassifiable and unserviceable libido, the non-sexual as opposed to a strictly defined sexuality. In its desiring form, it has no place in the social structure. Society burns its refuse : medieval society used to burn its homosexuals at the stake. Modern society has more rational methods of elimination. But "moral pollution" (to use Royer's phrase) seems to have the

57

same kind of staying power as industrial pollution: the machine produces a constantly rising flow of detritus, which it is increasingly incapable of bringing under control. Georges Henyer's dream is proving to be increasingly necessary, as well as increasingly impossible:

> "Doctors and magistrates are demanding for these mentally abnormal delinquents [homosexuals] a Social Defence law with high-security asylum facilities, where the sick could be treated and rehabilitated through psychotherapy and work."[29]

"Latent" and "patent" homosexuality

To present the oppression of homosexuality by the social machine as the manifestation of a paranoiac system of desire with homosexual roots presupposes the presence of desire in every institution. It is no longer sufficient to analyse society in terms of a conflict between conscious groups united by their interests (the classes). We must also recognise the existence, besides conscious (political) investments, of unconscious libidinal investments which sometimes conflict with the former (as in the case of communist activists).

At this point, we must recognise the analytic principles put forward by Deleuze and Guattari in *L'Anti-Oedipe*. It is not necessary to go through the Oedipal identifications in order to recognise the presence of desire in the social machine — not at a symbolic level, where only the family archetypes (for instance, the Father) would come into play, but at a direct level. This brings us back to the distinction between the molecular level of desire and the molar level of the great social machines. We can say, generally speaking, that the sublimation of homosexuality, as the basis for the functioning of the great social machines, corresponds to the oppression of the molecular by the molar. The latent homosexuality so beloved of psychoanalysts corresponds to the oppression of patent homosexuality; and we find the greatest charge of latent homosexuality in those social machines which are particularly anti-homosexual — the army, the school, the church, sport, etc. At the collective level, this sublimation is a means of transforming desire into the desire to repress.

58

3
"DISGUSTING PERVERTS . . ."

The psychiatrisation of homosexuality has not taken the place of penal repression : rather, the two things have gone hand in hand. Jailing homosexuals was sufficient at a time when sodomites were thought to be degenerates of the same type as the insane. Modern repression demands justifications, an interplay between legal guilt and the psychology of guilt. The judge's action is accompanied by the psychologist's understanding : the former stands for the positive institution of the judgement passed by normality, the latter implants guilt in the very heart of the individual. If repression is to be effective, the culprit must realise that it is necessary. The Law of the Father is vital to the fulfilment of the institutional laws. There is no real justice unless the accused has a guilty conscience.

This is how homosexuality becomes a neurosis. The homosexual is kith and kin to Nietzsche's Jew : the policeman in his head is the real medium of the uniformed policeman. No civilisation based exclusively on the domination by force of one sexual mode over all other possible modes can last : the collapse of religious belief calls for new, internal moral barriers. In this respect freudianism has played a key role : it is both the discoverer of the mechanisms of desire and the organiser of their control. Deleuze and Guattari compare the conditions of Freud's discovery to those of th⁻ capitalist discovery. The abstract general force at work in economic or sexual life is no sooner discovered than it is privatised into new alienating relations. Having discovered that labour is the basis of value, bourgeois political economy enchains it as private ownership of the means of production; Freud discovers the libido to be the basis of affective life and immediately enchains it as the Oedipal privatisation of the family. The first appearance of the libido is accompanied by the most amazing system of guilt-inducement ever invented.

At a time when capitalist individualisation is undermining the family by depriving it of its essential social functions, the Oedipus complex represents the internalisation of the family institution. The society in which divorce is most frequent — American society — is also the most Oedipalised. The Oedipalisation of homosexuality corresponds to an equivalent crisis in the social institutions. Simply fighting degeneracy is no longer enough : the meanings attached to punishment must be attached to the cure too.

The polymorphously perverse, bisexuality and non-human sex

What has become of Freud's discovery of the libido? How can his evidence, on which modern psychiatry is based, be used for the purposes of anti-homosexual repression? In the past it stood to reason that only one kind of sexuality existed, heterosexuality. It takes a considerable amount of distortion to turn recognition of the libido into the inducement of homosexual guilt.

And a particular amount of distortion is needed to turn desire into an absence rather than a production, to carve an absence in the very heart of desire, enabling it to be controlled. According to Deleuze and Guattari, it is the attribution of this absence in the form of the incest taboo that enables the Oedipus complex to be constructed. "Non-human sex", i.e. the impersonal flux of the libido, becomes the imaginary of the relations between persons within the family.

Freud expresses the fact that sex is non-human, and that desire is fundamentally undifferentiated and ignorant of the distinction between homosexuality and heterosexuality, by his use of the term "polymorphously perverse". It goes without saying that he simply borrowed the word "perverse" from the conventional linguistic distinction between the "normal person" and the "pervert" :

> "If I have described children as 'polymorphously perverse', I was only using a terminology that was generally current; no moral judgement was implied by the phrase. Psycho-

60

analysis has no concern whatever with such judgements of value."[30]

Young Törless's perplexities are a good illustration of the original polyvocality of desire. Törless doesn't know whether he desires anyone, Basini or Reiting. In fact, he simply desires.

In the work of Freud (following Wilhelm Fliess, whose conception is purely biological), the "polymorphously perverse" refers to the constitutional bisexuality of men and women — a concept which lies between biology and psychology, for desire ignores scientific divisions:

> "The most important perversion, homosexuality, hardly deserves the name. It comes down to a general disposition to bisexuality. . . . All human beings are capable of making a homosexual object-choice and have in fact made one in their unconscious."[31]

And again:

> "The disposition to perversions is itself no great rarity but must form a part of what passes as the normal constitution. . . . Psychoanalysis considers that a choice of an object independently of its sex — freedom to range equally over male and female objects — as it is found in childhood, in primitive states of society and early periods of history, is the original basis from which, as a result of restriction in one direction or the other, both the normal and the inverted types develop. Thus, from the point of view of psychoanalysis, the exclusive sexual interest felt by men for women is also a problem that needs elucidating and is not a self-evident fact based upon an attraction that is ultimately of a chemical nature."[32]

Both heterosexuality and homosexuality are the precarious outcome of a desire which knows no name. If the distinction between biology and psychology thus disappears, it is because desire knows nothing of the separation between body and mind upon which the personality is founded. Nevertheless, this kind of separation is the very life blood of psychiatry and psychoanalysis as an *institution*.

61

It is therefore no surprise to find that this is the expedient by which the misappropriation of Freud's thought has been organised. W. H. Gillespie[33] has made an extensive critique of the Freudian concept. "Freud based his concept of bisexuality to a large extent on biological and anatomical considerations" : reducing Freud to the level of Krafft-Ebing, i.e. to the level of a mechanical relationship between neatly defined psychological and biological elements, is the first step in the misappropriation. Gillespie's second step consists in using recent discoveries in chromosome research to demolish the biological basis previously attributed to Freud :

> "Some recent research has some relation to the 'discovery' . . . of the bisexuality of all cells. In a way, its demonstration goes against what Fliess believed. I refer to the chromosomal or nuclear sex, to the fact that it is now possible to distinguish sexual differences in the individual's somatic cells, differences which correspond in general to their manifest masculinity or femininity. . . . Undoubtedly, this discovery provides a serious argument against the bisexuality theory as understood by Freud."[34]

And further :

> "I among others, shall now strongly protest against any inclination to grant homosexuality a special place, outside the framework of perversions, simply on the grounds that it has biological and psychological foundations in bisexuality."[35]

This revision of Freud's theories strongly resembles revisions of Marx made in the light of modern technological discoveries. But one can only successfully revise what has previously been reduced to a revisable state. The chromosome theory appears to be less a biological "discovery" than an ideological regression : the homosexual becomes an accident of nature, an imbalance in the twenty-third pair of chromosomes. A similar imbalance, a similar natural "flaw" is used to account for the criminal personality (again, the inevitable association of the criminal with the homosexual). And since the number of "chromosomal" homosexuals is insignificant, Gillespie can refer homosexuality to psychiatry, to the Oedipal psychological operation; the whole of Freud's discovery then begins to slide into oblivion. This is what happens with those sciences which Fourier so rightly called "uncertain".

Hatred of woman

Desire, as an autonomous and polymorphous force, must disappear : in the eyes of the psychoanalytical institution, it must exist only as lack, or absence. It must always signify something, always relate to an object which will then become meaningful within the Oedipal triangulation. This is now the position of post-Freudian psychoanalysis, which is an institution of bourgeois society charged with controlling the libido.

Homosexuality is thus defined by its lack. It is no longer one of the accidental specifications of a polyvocal desire, but is assumed to signify hatred of woman, who is the only social sexual object. Heterosexuality is "full", as opposed to a homosexuality which lacks the essential object of desire. Certain ideological aspects of Freud's thought, which contrast in principle with his position on constitutional bisexuality, seem to sanction this stand. In his essay "On Narcissism: an Introduction", Freud distinguishes between two modes of existence of sexuality :

> "The individual himself regards sexuality as one of his own ends; whereas from another point of view he is an appendage to his germ-plasm, at whose disposal he puts his energies in return for a bonus of pleasure."[36]

This return to an essentially reproductive sexuality, which is merely episodic in Freud, becomes systematic with people such as Muldworf, the sexual theoretician who is on the payroll of the French Communist Party. Sexuality as reproduction (the family) takes over from desire as production. In Sartre's *Saint-Genêt* there is a description of this ideological certainty, as experienced by the "normal person" in contrast to the homosexual : he knows for sure that "woman will take care of everything — of our pleasure, and of the species."

Thus "woman", who otherwise, as such, has no place in society, who is referred to as the *only* social sexual object, is also the absence attributed to the homosexual relationship. And the homosexual relationship is therefore not a partial manifestation of desire coexisting with heterosexuality, but a relationship in which reproduction is absent. Stekel gives us a good example of this kind of reductionism. He accepts the theory of bisexuality, but then puts the focus on the alleged elimination of woman in male homosexuality; he believes that the homosexual is denied access to woman because of his family history. In his chapter on "Impotence and Criminality", he writes:

> "Why is the homosexual impotent with women? The question appears naïve. Most physicians would reply: because he has no libido with women and only desires men. It is just this point of view which I so energetically demonstrated in *Auto-Erotism*, and demonstrated that the homosexual only repressed his heterosexual component because he harbours an attitude of sadism (with hatred) towards womanhood. The conviction to which I have come is as follows: the homosexual parapathy is a flight to the same sex motivated by an attitude of sadism towards the opposite sex."[37]

We can see here how psychiatric thought can start out by accepting bisexuality, but proceeds to account for one of the forms of sexual relationship by fear of the other form. Homosexuality is seen as essentially neurotic, and this neurosis is related to the hatred of woman. Desire is defined by its absence; absence and fear are the preconditions of the Oedipal construction. Fear of man or woman, or fear of the mother or father — the two explanations are usually concurrent:

> "Thus, one of the most common causes liable to drive an individual to homosexuality is the fear of man — the paternal image — leading to withdrawal into passive female identification with the mother, in order to escape the dreaded aggression."[38]

As we can see, the contradictions are ignored. What matters is *fear,* and we shall meet this later in connection with castration and with the phallus, in its role as the dispenser of meaning between the sexes.

The oedipalisation of homosexuality

Homosexuality now takes its place in the neurotic family romance, in the construction of Oedipus. This is only proper: the Oedipus complex is the only effective means of controlling the libido. Stages need to be built, a pyramidal construction that will enclose homosexual desire within the three sides of the triangle. Freud frequently attacked Hirschfeld's "third sex" theory. As against the liberalism which accepts homosexuality only on condition that it is enclosed within a different sex, Freud asserted the universality of homosexual desire, as a translation of the polymorphously perverse. But no sooner had he discovered the universality of this "perversion" than he enclosed it, not geographically but historically, within the Oedipal system. The "Leonardo da Vinci" text, is in this respect, self-explanatory. Freud presents two facts about male homosexuality as unquestionable: mother fixation, and the fact that in Freud's words "every human being is capable of making a homosexual object-choice" and has made it, either keeping to it or shielding himself from it.

We can account for the possibility of neurosis here, i.e. a "retreat" of the repressed to a unisexual choice. But how do we account for the fact that homosexuality is the only unisexual choice that is condemned as neurotic?

Castration and narcissism

"Leonardo da Vinci and a Memory of his Childhood" was Freud's first step towards a new way of analysing homosexuality, and was an immediate success. Leonardo's homosexuality is centred on the "vulture phantasy", a child sucking a vulture's tail. The child is Leonardo, the vulture's tail is both the mother's breast and the penis. Freud sees it as a sign of the painter's passive homosexuality; it springs from the disgust aroused by his discovery of the absence of a penis in the woman, which he attributes to a wound or an ablation. Enter

65

castration. Freud's struggle against the "third sex" theory becomes the universalisation of the Oedipus complex. The phallus, the dispenser of meaning, is experienced by the little girl as the absence of a penis, and by the little boy as the fear of losing it, i.e. as castration anxiety. Guilty conscience makes its appearance, a form of guilt in which subject and object become divided.

According to this view, the passive homosexual — and it is essentially he who is under discussion, to such an extent that he summarises all homosexuality by himself — is characterised by his fear of the absence of a penis or his fear of losing it. He is also incapable of breaking away from the mother, for she is full of the meaning which is absent in him.

Narcissism assumes its full significance here. The choice of a sexual object external to the individual becomes a necessity, an anaclitic choice. Freud wrote "On Narcissism: an Introduction" in order to analyse this stage of desire, which is itself an absence, inasmuch as it presupposes a later stage:

> "We have discovered, especially clearly in people whose libidinal development has suffered some disturbance, such as perverts and homosexuals, that in their later choice of love objects they have taken as a model not their mother but their own selves."[39]

By making his anaclitic choice on a narcissistic basis, the homosexual is in a way deprived of an object. Freud similarly defined woman by the absence in her of a phallus: besides, according to Freud, there is a basic narcissism in woman, and the homosexual inherits some of her characteristics.

Narcissism is objectless desire, and therefore close to the original libido, and is also this same desire as the absence of a history of the libido. It is the end of the unconsciousness of non-human sex, and the beginning of personalised and imaginary Oedipal sexuality. That is why it stands at the knot of the Oedipalisation of homosexual desire. The body-in-pieces anxiety, the castration anxiety, can obviously only be subsequent to Lacan's "mirror stage". To identify oneself, to bind the organs into a single person, means to leave behind the polymorphously perverse, or rather to initiate the perversity of

66

the polymorphous. Certainly, the whole person created by the mirror stage comes chronologically second; but actually it comes first, because it is that person who retrospectively gives the first stage its meaning, and all the "component drives" are then integrated in a bodily unity, according to the principle that the form is pre-existent to the parts. The whole person becomes the absence which is present in the component objects. The search for a counterpart similar to oneself presupposes the existence of the similar and the different. The narcissistic stage is the process by which the unnamable desire becomes identified with the similar or the different, with heterosexuality or homosexuality. Of course, narcissism is more or less equally distributed between heterosexuality and homosexuality — which is also the case, as we have seen, with the neurosis that is born of unisexuality. But as though by chance, just as neurosis becomes homosexuality's mode of existence, so too does narcissism become the theme of its operation.

Guilt pushes its way into the absence; narcissism and homosexuality supply the field of sublimation with its preferential object, to the point where we can truthfully say that sublimation is simply homosexuality in its historical family truth. Freud writes at the end of "On Narcissism: an Introduction": "The liberation of the homosexual libido . . . is transformed into a sense of guilt (social anxiety)."[40] If the root of narcissism and homosexuality, i.e. of narcissism as the agent operating the distinction between homosexuality and heterosexuality, turns into social anxiety, then the neurotic Oedipal ego is closely bound to it: "A considerable amount of [a person's] homosexual libido . . . is in this way turned back into the ego,"[41] that is, into the moral conscience produced by the intervention of parents and educators.

What is described is at the same time constructed: we only find in the Oedipalised homosexual libido what we have put there in the first place. In this sense, the analysis of homosexuality is at the same time the construction of the whole family romance, where it will have to go on living whether it likes it or not.

Oedipus or the chromosomes?

In general Greek mythology, or at least the psychoanalysts' version of it, does not get on well with homosexuals. In the imaginary of psychoanalysis, a pederastic society such as that of the Greeks uses its myths to supply weapons against the very things which those myths help people to think. Greek love and Oedipal love merge into one. The heterosexual imperialism of the family sneaks its own neurotic meanings into homosexuality. "Perversion" is then no longer the negative of neurosis; homosexual perversion can dispense with the inverted commas. The lure of the imaginary encompasses the entire libidinal field.

The image of the mother takes the place of the breast, and elusive desire, with its innumerable possibilities of plugging in, becomes fixed. The word "fixation" clearly reveals the considerable effort made by Oedipal psychoanalysis. The "mother fixation" from which Leonardo suffered (at least, Freud states that he suffered from it) binds the unconscious, names the unnamable, places the homosexual in his position as one person facing another, as an individual who is both irresponsible and responsible for his own irresponsibility. The mother fixation is the strongest bond between homosexual desire and the normal world, the safest kind of normalisation. It has never faltered since the moment Freudianism first appeared, and has in fact grown considerably, along with the extensive popularisation of analytic themes. The *produced* homosexual has only to come and occupy the place reserved for him, to play the part programmed for him, and he does it with enthusiasm and even asks for more. The analytic explanation is popular, of course; and it isn't because Freud is only read by a few specialists that the influence of Oedipus stops there. There is only one way of answering the question "Why homosexuality?" besides the chromosomal explanation, and that is to use vulgar analysis.

Moreover, they blend into each other. In 1962, *France-Dimanche* published a series of articles on homosexuality which held whole families in breathless attention for a month and a half. The headline proclaimed, "The truth about homosexuality: a series of articles which all mothers must read". Why mothers? Because *France-Dimanche* is well aware that it is they who exert the most effective control of the homosexual libido, and that it would be a good thing to intensify this control. Under the sub-heading "Who is responsible?" one of the articles concluded:

> "A Swiss psychiatrist goes straight to the point: according to him, in seventy per cent of cases, it is the parents who are responsible for their children's homosexuality, and particularly the mother! ... *Stress the mother's responsibility, however astounding it may seem. Too many mothers wish in their heart of hearts for their sons to be homosexual."* (Emphasis in the original.)

One of the strongest Oedipal arguments is the notion of parental responsibility as a weapon of universal responsibility: "Oedipus is the notion of an adult paranoiac before it is the infantile feeling of a neurotic", write Deleuze and Guattari. Paranoiacs beget neurotics, heterosexuality gives rise to homosexuality. Everything starts in the head of the father or mother, because there has to be a beginning: thou shalt desire thy mother, and thy mother shall desire on thy behalf. And anyway, that is just what you wanted when you were sucking the breast, though you did not know it at the time. The ego is the true unconscious of desire, not desire the unconscious of the ego.

The homosexual judge

We have already mentioned Schreber in the first chapter; with Freud, we recognised his case as a compensatory paranoia of the unfulfilled but insufficiently repressed homosexual libido. Schreber is at the same time a paranoiac and a neurotic; his delusion is general, in that it produces its content and its interpretation at the same time. Schreber's homosexuality is translated into the terms of Oedipal guilt-inducement in the course of its own production: Schreber, God's woman, is also the world's redeemer. His transformation into a woman is the extraordinary sacrifice by which he saves the world. The justificatory paranoia stretches homosexual desire between the two extremes of sacrifice and pleasure: elevation towards Godhead and acceptance of the lowliest social and sexual condition, the woman's. His

69

relationship with Dr Flechsig is experienced both as fear and desire, the fear of rape and the desire of rape. Passive homosexuality, i.e. Homosexuality, is experienced only at the price of castration; to be homosexual is to have been castrated by the father. The homosexual receives his meaning from the sex-dispensing phallus. Castration/sacrifice: the expiatory gift of masculinity.

The two opposing poles which constitute Schreber's paranoia are the same as those which organise the heterosexual relation: woman is either a goddess or a charwoman, an archetype or a sexual object. Schreber experiences homosexuality as a heterosexual would imagine it to be experienced. In a way, Sartre's Gênet (for Genêt belongs to Sartre as surely as Schreber belongs to Freud) also affirms the sacrificial role of passive homosexuality. The chains which in Genêt's novel *The Miracle of the Rose* are transformed into roses reveal the bond between the sublime and the abominable: we only sacrifice what we value. Homosexuality is redeemed by the absolute gift — the total sacrifice, where pleasure is what is prohibited. Sartre says that Divine, in *Our Lady of the Flowers,* is a character who seeks pleasure secretly. Divine's only little secret is that his Oedipus complex is one of Redemption through degradation. It is a kind of enlightened homosexuality, where God passes judgement after certain rites of initiation: according to Father Oraison, homosexuality is evidence of God, revealing Him all the more because of its degradation. As such, it is fragile and dear to God's heart; in a way, it represents the second coming.

Thomas Mann's Aschenbach is caught similarly between a putrefying Venice and the memory of his ancestors:

"... In consternation he asked himself what path was this on which he had set his foot. Like most other men of parts and attainments, he had an aristocratic interest in his forbears, and when he achieved success he liked to think he had gratified them, compelled their admiration and regard."

Aschenbach comes from a titled line, and he experiences his membership of it as a paranoia of filiation; his sacrifice to Tadzio is magnified all the more by it. Anyone who can be so completely engrossed with the distinction of his line and with his forbears must agree to be reborn in the worst possible condition : that of an old homosexual pressing his attentions on a young boy. To descend from the highest condition to this level, where the sexual object totally dominates in a deified form : here lies the homosexual assumption. Aschenbach's passion reluctantly takes a form similar to his passion for classical culture, Greek statues and Platonic quotations. This transfigures and redeems the homosexual condition, and just as Genêt's chains become roses, Aschenbach is transformed :

> "He leaned back, with hanging arms, quivering from head to foot, and quite unmanned he whispered the hackneyed phrase of love and longing — impossible in these circumstances, absurd, abject, ridiculous enough, yet sacred too, and not unworthy of honour even here : 'I love you!' "

It is through the mediation of desire that the sacred comes into its own. Homosexual love is as miraculous as it is troubled, and Proust conveys this in *Contre Sainte-Beuve* :

> "Nature, as it has done for certain animals and flowers in which the organs of love are so badly placed that they almost never find pleasure, has certainly made them no gift with regard to love."

Homosexual encounters become a real miracle, a kind of predestination that is both splendid and accursed.

Of course, we are giving these delusions merely the interpretation they invite. In *L'Anti-Oedipe* it is rightly observed that Schreber's phantasy of the sun whose rays visit the new Virgin can only be seen as an image of the father if the cosmology of desire is reduced to the level of a family phantasy. It is because homosexual desire is too conspicuous, because the Oedipal cloak is an absolute precondition for its social appearance, that these delusions are at the same time their own interpretation. Vautrin drags Rubempré out of the dark, he forms him socially. According to Pasche, in Balzac's *Splendeur et misère des courtesanes* when Vautrin brings Rubempré up from nothing, he constitutes him socially. Pasche writes :

> "We get the impression that for Vautrin it was a matter of

71

altering, redoing, interfering with, parodying and ultimately destroying the divine opus, the father's creature."[42]

Homosexuality is a parody, it plays Judas to Christianity's Oedipus : that is its only social status. Senatspräsident Schreber, the chairman of a court of justice, can become homosexual only if in the drift of desire he is held fast by the chain of father fixation. Their is no perversion without shame.

Cure: the infernal cycle

The important question is not even whether to make love with men or not, but to be a good homosexual. If you cannot sublimate, then be conscious of your own abject state. Know that there is a heaven and hell of sexuality; if you choose hell, on your own head be it. In order to bind homosexuality, Oedipal psychiatry emprisons it between an "up" and a "down", a "to be cured or not to be cured", a perverse homosexuality and a neurotic homosexuality which reflect each other.

It must not be assumed that the cure ideology has disappeared. It is one of the two constants of the alternative, each of which would have no meaning without the other. And whatever liberal opinion may be on the matter, doctors continue to practise the cure of homosexuality.* Adler, who represents the true American analytic practice, writes in conclusion to his work on homosexuality : "Psychic therapy may result in cure or improvement; nevertheless, this is not going to be an easy task." (Had he not also written previously : "Besides, we had forgotten the numerous cases of homosexuality which have finally achieved heterosexuality" ?) Heterosexuality must remain the forbidden but ever-present Eden, the dream of total social reconciliation :

"It may be clearly inferred from our accounts that homosexuality must be considered a failure in the individual's

---

* Cure by castration is practised in the USA[44] by electric shock treatment, by hormone injections, by chemotherapy, by lobotomy, and last but not least, by behavioural therapy — "rewards" and "penalties", with injections or electric shocks accompanying the projection of nude photographs.[45]

social education; whereas education must normally tend to arouse the individual's spirit of collective co-operation."[43]

Heterosexual ideology needs both an innate or perverse homosexuality and a diseased homosexuality at the same time. Predestination and sin are coexistent.

To be cured is to assume your Oedipus complex; not to be cured is to assume your homosexuality and to assume the Oedipus complex in another form. The popular *France-Dimanche* survey pursued the same theme : one article was headed, "Yes, doctors can cure homosexuality". It is possible, they explain, to cure one third of homosexual cases with the help of psychological treatment. Homosexuality thus inherits the enclosing characteristics of the Oedipus complex and its double-bind game : bind up the two ends, leaving either transgression or obedience as the only way out. To accept homosexuality involves taking on "the problems of the homosexual" which the social imaginary imposes on one; to reject homosexuality is to accept oneself as normal.

Reactionary psychiatry denounces the pervert as someone who refuses to be cured, liberal psychiatry pities those who cannot assume their own selves. The *France-Dimanche* survey gives us a mixture of both : yes homosexuals can be cured, and yes it is better to accept yourself than to run away from yourself. But whether you choose acceptance or flight, you are yourself. If you accept yourself, you will please your mother and displease your father. If you do not accept yourself, the contrary will be true. Father and mother are already at the two vertices of the triangle; you must now take your place at the third. The most simplistic kind of characterisation then becomes valid : if you are feminine, you will be sensitive — an artist or a hairdresser, according to your class (each class possesses an imaginary of its own possibilities). Or, if you are incapable of assuming this role, then neurosis will be your fate. You will no longer know who you are, but you will desire to be somebody :

> "This is the *either/or* rule in the differentiating function of the incest taboo. Here is mummy, here is daddy, and you are over there. Stay where you belong."[46]

In the eyes of the law a potential culprit, in the eyes of psychiatry

73

the homosexual is potentially sick. His fate depends on his ability to display remorse at not being heterosexual, and to be a glorious and miserable exception.

Homosexuality and shame

It is not enough to say that shame and homosexuality are closely connected. One only exists in the movement of the other. Proust entitled the famous section which occurs both in *Contre Sainte-Beuve* and at the beginning of *Sodom and Gomorrah,* "The Accursed Race". It is easy to see why he changed the original phrase, "The Race of Queens"[ᶻ]. To the public, homosexuality is the concentrate of the shameful little Oedipal secret.

The imaginary of the public continues to focus on the big vice trials and scandals in the gossip columns. The imaginary of homosexuality at this level is so far from the immediate practices of desire that no one who has experienced such practices at college or in the army would dream of drawing a comparison between the two. He would never think for a moment that he belonged to a "race upon which a curse weighs and which must live amid falsehood and perjury, because it knows the world to regard as a punishable and a scandalous, as an inadmissible thing, its desire, that which constitutes for every human creature the greatest happiness in life."[47] Homosexuality is no longer a relation of desire, but an ontological standpoint. Proust's homosexual, as he appears in *Sodom and Gomorrah,* lives in the complicity which exists between abnormals. The imaginary of the mirror obscures all social relations :

> "Friends without friendships, despite all those which their charm, frequently recognised, inspires and their hearts, often generous, would gladly feel; but can we describe as friendship those relations which flourish only by virtue of a lie and from which the first outburst of confidence and sincerity in which they might be tempted to indulge would make them be expelled with disgust, unless they are dealing with an impartial, that is to say a sympathetic mind, which however in that case, misled with regard to them by a conventional psychology, will suppose to spring from the vice

74

the very affection that is most alien to it, just as certain judges assume and are more inclined to pardon murder in inverts and treason in Jews for reasons derived from original sin and racial predestination."[48]

The homosexual exists first of all in the normal person's paranoia; the judge knows him to be guilty, just as the doctor knows him to be sick. In Sartre's words :

"Narcissism, they'll say. But narcissism no more comes first than pride or homosexuality. First, one must be guilty."[49]

The myth of the "accursed race" and the myth of narcissism beget each other. *Contre Sainte-Beuve* contains the wonderful portrait of "a young boy who, mocked by his brother and his friends, was strolling alone along the beach . . . still too pure to believe that a desire like his could exist outside books, unable to think that the scenes of debauchery we identify it with could have any bearing on him, putting them as we do in the same category as theft and murder."[50] Homosexual encounters are fixed by the members of a secret fraternity which is visible only through the signs they exchange and which, for a brief moment, troubles the limpid serenity of the social structure. It is a fraternity in which

"Signs . . . indicate one of his congeners to the beggar in the street, in the great nobleman whose carriage door he is closing, to the father in the suitor for his daughter's hand, to him who has sought healing, absolution, defence, in the doctor, the priest, the barrister to whom he has had recourse; all of them obliged to protect their own secret but having their part in a secret shared with the others."[51]

A nineteenth-century Chief of the Sûreté, Louis Canler, outlined the following typology of homosexuals, whom he calls *les honteuses* ("disgusting ladies") :

"*Les honteuses* reject and dismiss everything which could draw attention to them. Besides, since they are dressed like everybody else, nothing could betray them, unless it be their feminine voice. This group consists of people belonging to all classes of society, with no exception."[52]

75

This fraternity scents out its members; it is intolerable to normal people because it is self-recognised, or rather self-confessed. All relationships between the homosexual and his circle are trapped in the problematic of confession, in a guilty situation where desire is criminal and is experienced as such. And just as Jews can easily be anti-semitic, homosexuals can easily be anti-homosexual. "It was clear from his words that Monsieur de Charlus considered sexual inversion as threatening to young people as prostitution is to women" :[53] homosexuality is a sickness of being because of its inability to become a being.

These extracts from Proust are an inducement for us to read Charlus in the Oedipal sense. But at the same time Proust's work reveals something of the informality of desire, although it is reduced to illegibility and overlaid by his relation to his "little mother", from which, we must remember, the text on homosexuality in *Contre Sainte-Beuve* sprang. Proust, both as a person and as a writer, is someone who tells pretty tales to his mother as a way of confessing his homosexuality. *Contre Sainte-Beuve* is constructed around a "conversation with mother" in which the Oedipus complex reaches the height of absurdity :

> "I am only a sensitive person, tortured by anxiety. I look at mother, I put my arms around her.
> 'What is my silly boy thinking about, some nonsense I suppose?'
> 'I would be so happy if I could stop seeing anyone else but you.'
> 'Don't say this, my pet . . .'
> I am happy with my mother."[54]

However, alongside the family romance of homosexual confession and (in Deleuze and Guattari's words) the abject "desire to be loved", *A la recherche du temps perdu* contains what we may call the "language of flowers". If it is true that the grandmother is the Oedipus complex squared, then Charlus's words to the narrator, "So you couldn't care less about your grandmother, eh, you little rogue?", become the introduction to a different reading of *Sodom,* one which adds weight to the introductory passage in which Charlus buzzes around Jupien like an insect around a flower. Of course the language of flowers can be

76

seen, as with Genêt's roses, as the transfiguration of the base into the sublime. But it is the biological aspect of this love which holds Proust's attention. He is like a child passionately absorbed in watching animals mate:

> "I knew that this expectancy was no more passive than in the male flower, whose stamens had spontaneously curved so that the insect might more easily receive their offering."[55]

And he states it explicitly:

> "My reflexions had followed a tendency which I shall describe in due course, and I had already drawn from the visible stratagems of flowers a conclusion that bore upon a whole unconscious element of literary work."[56]

The scene between Charlus and Jupien is neither comic nor tragic; it is, writes Proust, "stamped with a strangeness, or if you like a naturalness, the beauty of which steadily increased."[57] And the beauty of the expressions on the faces of Charlus and Jupien comes from the fact that they "did not . . . seem to be intended to lead to anything further."[58] The "stratagems of the flowers" lie in the non-signifying character of this scene: it is self-explanatory. The great phallic signifier is missing. These flowers and insects have no sex; they are the very *machine* of sexual *desire*.

No more fraternities, no more secrets on a sunny afternoon in some courtyard.

To strip homosexual desire of its moral Oedipal cloak would involve suppressing or rather bypassing, what "writers" such as Proust represent. The Proust-Gide-Peyrefitte sequence is reminiscent of the Freud-Adler-*France-Dimanche* sequence. Proust is as deeply involved in the Oedipal reduction of homosexuality and homosexual sensitivity as Freud is in the analysis and "understanding" of it. They both make desire and the plugging in of desire appear without rhyme or reason. They both know the secret of the discourses which imprison desire in myriad Oedipal nets. And while Proust is probably one of the first people to speak of a homosexual movement, he concludes the first chapter of *Sodom and Gomorrah* with this warning:

> "But I have thought it as well here to utter a provisional

warning against the lamentable error of proposing (just as people have encouraged a Zionist movement) to create a Sodomist movement and to rebuild Sodom."[59]

A warning against what the unchaining of desire might lead to, but also : no need to rebuild a lost homeland, a perverse territorialisation of desire — let it be. Proust is as ambiguous as narcissism; he paves the way for the accursed race as much as for its liberation.

4

CAPITALISM, THE FAMILY AND THE ANUS

The chief ideological modes of thinking about homosexuality date back to the turn of the century; they are thus connected, though not mechanically so, with the advance of Western capitalism. They are a perverse re-territorialisation, in a world which is tending towards de-territorialisation. The purpose of these reconstituted axiomatic modes of thinking is to replace the failing codes. We have escaped from hellfire into psychological hell. Capitalist ideology's strongest weapon is its transformation of the Oedipus complex into a social characteristic, an internalisation of oppression which is left free to develop, whatever the political conditions. The anti-capitalist movement can often be pro-family, and indeed anti-homosexual. The apologetic type of homosexual literature generally deals with homosexuality by way of judicious reference to the Greeks, and this return to phantasmatical origins is suited to the perversity of re-territorialisation : in such literature we find no hint of a society in which there might be free expression of a homosexual desire that could be opposed to our present society.

After capitalist decoding has taken place, there is no room for any form of homosexual integration other than that of perverse axiomatisation.

The place of the family is now less in the institutions and more in the mind. The family is the place where sexual pleasure is legal, though no longer in the sense that everybody has to marry in order to take their pleasure within the law; far from putting an end to the exclusive function of reproductive heterosexuality, the actual dissolution by capitalism of the functions of the family has turned the family into the rule inhabiting every individual under free competition. This individual does not replace the family, he prolongs its farcical games. The decoding of the fluxes of pleasure is accompanied by their axiomatisation, just as the disappearance of the journeyman's apprenticeship and the discovery of labour as value go hand in hand with private ownership of the means of production.

Here we find the solution to the apparent contradiction that this society appears to be increasingly sexualised yet is more deep-seatedly repressive than any other: its sexualisation, and homosexuality in particular, is placed under the sign of guilt or transgression. The more is expected from desire, the less it is allowed to express itself, nor has it ever before been associated with so many images. The advertising media flood us with the images of naked young *ephebi*; the meaning, however, is: "What we desire has already been translated into a marketable transgression". Countless discussions daily restore the family meanings and induce artificial guilt even among young people who live at the margins of society. Freud's dubious success among young revolutionaries is indicative of the guilt-inducing power of the Oedipus complex.

We have been speaking alternately about "homosexual desire" and the perverse situation of homosexuality. The social manifestation of "homosexual desire" is perverse, while that same desire is at the same time an expression of the unformulated nature of the libido. If our society really is experiencing what Marcuse believes to be a growing homosexualisation, then that is because it is becoming perverted, because liberation is immediately re-territorialised. The emergence of unformulated desire is too destructive to be allowed to become more than a fleeting phenomenon which is immediately surrendered to a recuperative interpretation. Capitalism turns its homosexuals into failed "normal people", just as it turns its working class into an imitation of the middle class. This imitation middle class provides the best illustration of bourgeois values (the proletarian family); failed "normal people" emphasise the normality whose values they assume (fidelity, love, psychology, etc.).

Homosexual desire has two aspects: one is desire, the other is homosexuality. There can only be "growing homosexualisation", in Marcuse's words, if there is also a more thorough enclosure of desire within a play of images. It is also true that our world of social relationships is largely built on the sublimation of homosexuality. The social world exploits homosexual desire more than it exploits any other kind, by converting libidinal energy into a system of representation. If one wants to attack the representations and to rid the libidinal energy of its moral cloak where homosexuality is concerned, then one must first reveal the confrontation between the social ideology and the strength of a desire which, as in the case of Charlus and Jupien, is so tightly welded as not to leave the slightest crack for interpretation to enter.

There are thus two sides to what we mean by the term "homosexual desire" : an ascent towards sublimation, the superego and social anxiety, and a descent towards the abyss of non-personalised and uncodified desire. It would perhaps be a good thing to take the opposite path to Gide, and follow the descending line as far as it goes. This leads us to desire as the plugging in of organs subject to no rule or law.

The phallic signifier and the sublimated anus

The world of Oedipal sexuality is deprived of a free plugging in of organs, of the relations of direct pleasure. There is just one organ — a purely sexual organ — at the centre of the Oedipal triangulation, the "One" which determines the position of the three elements of the triangle. This is the organ which constructs absence; it is the "despotic signifier", in relation to which the situations of the whole person are created. It is the detached, complete object which plays the same role in our society's sexuality as money does in the capitalist economy: the fetish, the true universal reference-point for all activity. It is responsible for the allocation of both absence and presence : the little girl's penis-envy, the little boy's castration anxiety.

Ours is a phallic society, and the quantity of possible pleasure is determined in relation to the phallus. All sexual acts have an "aim" which gives them their meaning; they are organised into preliminary caresses which will eventually crystallise in the necessary ejaculation, the touchstone of pleasure. It is in this sense that the relationship between Charlus and Jupien is "aimless". The phallus draws on libidinal energy in the same way that money draws on labour.

81

Our society is so phallic that the sexual act without ejaculation is felt to be a failure. After all, what do men care if — as is often the case — the woman remains frigid and feels no pleasure? Phallic pleasure is the raison d'être of heterosexuality, whichever sex is involved.

Ours is a phallocratic society, inasmuch as social relationships as a whole are constructed according to a hierarchy which reveals the transcendence of the great signifier. The schoolmaster, the general and the departmental manager are the father-phallus; everything is organised according to the pyramidal mode, by which the Oedipal signifier allocates the various levels and identifications. The body gathers round the phallus like society round the chief. Both those in whom it is absent and those who obey it belong to the kingdom of the phallus: this is the triumph of Oedipus.

Whereas the phallus is essentially social, the anus is essentially private. If phallic transcendence and the organisation of society around the great signifier are to be possible, the anus must be privatised in individualised and Oedipalised persons:

> "The first organ to be privatised, to be excluded from the social field, was the anus. It gave privatisation its model, just as money was expressing the new abstract status of the fluxes."[60]

The anus has no social position except sublimation. The functions of this organ are truly private; they are the site of the formation of the person. The anus expresses privatisation itself. The analytic case-history (and we cannot help seeing "anal" in "analytic") presupposes that the anal stage is transcended so that the genital stage may be reached. But the anal stage is necessary if detachment from the phallus is to take place. In fact sublimation is exercised on the anus as on no other organ, in the sense that the anus is made to progress from the lowest to the highest point: anality is the very movement of sublimation itself.

Freud sees the anal stage as the stage of formation of the person. The anus has no social desiring function left, because all its functions have become excremental: that is to say, chiefly private. The great act of capitalist decoding is accompanied by

82

the constitution of the individual; money, which must be privately owned in order to circulate, is indeed connected with the anus, in so far as the anus is the most private part of the individual. The constitution of the private, individual, "proper" person is "of the anus"; the constitution of the public person is "of the phallus".

The anus does not enjoy the same ambivalence as the phallus, i.e. its duality as penis and Phallus. Of course, to expose one's penis is a shameful act, but it is also a glorious one, inasmuch as it displays some connection with the Great Social Phallus. Every man possesses a phallus which guarantees him a social role; every man has an anus which is truly his own, in the most secret depths of his own person. The anus does not exist in a social relation, since it forms precisely the individual and therefore enables the division between society and the individual to be made. Schreber is severely handicapped by no longer being able to shit on his own : one does not shit in company. Lavatories are the only place where one is alone behind locked doors. There is no anal pornography (apart from anti-social exceptions). The anus is over-invested individually because its investment is withdrawn socially.

All the libidinal energy directed towards the anus is diverted so that the social field may be organised along lines of sublimation and the private person. "The entire Oedipus complex is anal",[41] and the desiring use of the anus is inversely proportional to social anality. Your excrement is yours and yours alone : what you do with it is your own business. Among the organs, the anus plays the kind of role that narcissism plays in relation to the constitution of the individual : it is the source of energy giving rise to the social sexual system and the oppression which this system imposes upon desire.

Homosexuality and the anus

It may be said that homosexuals are not alone in making a desiring use of the anus. However, I did mention that there are some anti-social exceptions. Georges Bataille, although heterosexual, perceived the peculiarly repressed nature of this zone of the bourgeois body; however, Bataille cannot be considered as an adequate expression of social sexuality, but rather as its extreme limit. No anal pornography, did we say? Heterosexual pornography certainly sets great store by women's buttocks. But the woman's buttocks and breasts are a plenum, a fully-occupied space around which the man may cup his hands, whereas the anus remains an intimate vacuum, the site of a mysterious and private kind of production: that is, excremental production.

The desiring use of the anus made by homosexuals is the chief, if not the exclusive one. Only homosexuals make such constant libidinal use of this zone. The only part of Charlus's body we know something about, besides his face, is this one, when Jupien tells him, "What a fat arse you have"; and certainly the transformation which takes place in our minds at this point with regard to Charlus is far greater than anything we can glean from all the psychological subtleties of Proust's description of him. Homosexual desire challenges anality-sublimation because it restores the desiring use of the anus. Schreber forgets how to shit at the point when his resistance to his own homosexual libido is partly breaking down. Homosexuality primarily means anal homosexuality, sodomy.

At the end of his article "The Nosology of Male Homosexuality", Ferenczi makes a statement of great significance:

> "The reason why every kind of affection between men is proscribed is not clear. It is thinkable that the sense of cleanliness which has been so specially reinforced in the past few centuries, i.e. the *repression of anal erotism,* has provided the strongest motive in this direction; for homo-erotism, even the most sublimated, stands in a more or less unconscious associative connection with paederastia, i.e. an anal erotic activity."[62]

There is a certain "kind of affection" — or rather a desiring relation as opposed to its sublimated form, friendship — which anal cleanliness does not permit, "anal cleanliness" being the formation in the child of the small responsible person; and there is a relation between "private cleanliness" and "private ownership" [*propreté privée* and *propriété privée*] which is not merely an association of words but something inevitable. Ferenczi also

84

wrote a paper on "Stimulation of the Anal Erotogenic Zone as a Precipitating Factor in Paranoia" (1911). The patient was a forty-five-year-old peasant whose social activity was notable for its extraordinary zeal : he displayed a great interest in parish affairs, in which he took an active part. After an operation for an anal fistula, he took no further part in the village affairs and fell victim to persecutory paranoia. For Ferenczi, the relationship between paranoia and homosexuality involved the following line of reasoning :

> "The necessity for manipulation of his rectum by males (physicians) might have stimulated the patient's hitherto latent or sublimated homosexual tendencies."[63]

The paranoia sprang from the resurgence of the homosexual libido, which until then had been successfully sublimated in friendship for the village men and in the patient's important public role. Ferenczi inferred from this that the disappearance of the patient's anal fixation would lead to his recovery; in other words, "the patient might recover his capacity for sublimation (for intellectualised homosexuality in a community sense)".[64]

It follows that the anal homosexual drive only has the right to emerge sublimated. The repression of the desiring function of the anus, in Schreber's case as in that of Ferenczi's peasant, is the precondition for their playing an important public role, for preserving their "goods" (in the legal sense), their property, their individuality and their anal cleanliness. Control of the anus is the precondition of taking responsibility for property. The ability to "hold back" or to evacuate the faeces is the necessary moment of the constitution of the self. "To forget oneself" is the most ridiculous and distressing kind of social accident there is, the ultimate outrage to the human person. In contemporary society, total degradation is to live in one's own waste, which only prison or the concentration camp can force us to do. "To forget oneself" is to risk joining up, through the flux of excrement, with the non-differentiation of desire. Homosexuality is connected with the anus, and anality with our civilisation. Albert Moll, a disciple of Krafft-Ebing, wrote in 1891 :

> "Men with homosexual tendencies have generally masturbated since their earliest age, only instead of rubbing their

85

penis, they introduce any sort of object into their anus."[65]
Note the words "any sort". Certainly he regards whatever the
object is as a substitute phallus. But we also find here an acknow-
ledgement that there is an independent anal orgasm, unrelated to
ejaculation. This anal orgasm has only brief moments of social
existence, on those occasions where it is able to take advantage
of a temporary disappearance of guilt-inducing repression.

The anus is so well hidden that it forms the subsoil of the
individual, his "fundamental" core. It is his own property, as the
thief's grandfather explains in Darien's *Le voleur* ("your thumb
belongs to you so you must not suck it; you must protect what
is yours").[66] Your anus is so totally yours that you must not use
it: keep it to yourself. The phallus is to be found everywhere,
the popularisation of psychoanalysis having made it the common
signifier of all social images. But who would think of interpret-
ing Schreber's sun, not as the father-phallus, but as a cosmic
anus?

We only see our anus in the mirror of narcissism, face to face,
or rather back to front, with our own clean, private little person.
The anus only exists as something which is socially elevated and
individually debased; it is torn between faeces and poetry,
between the shameful little secret and the sublimated. To reject
the conversion of anal libidinal energy into the paranoia mechanism would mean to risk loss of identity, and to discard the
perverse re-territorialisation which has been forced upon homosexuality.

Deleuze and Guattari's remark, "only the mind is capable of
shitting," means that only the mind is capable of producing
excremental matter, that only sublimation is capable of situating
the anal. Our anal sexuality is enclosed somewhere between
the sublime, rarefied air of the mind and the deep excremental
swamp of the anus. Here too the double-bind is the rule, the
simultaneous production of two conflicting messages which are,
however, coherent in their successful binding of the production
of desire.

Homosexuality and the loss of identity

Sex is the first digit in the French national identity card number.

86

Neurosis consists first of all in the impossibility of knowing (which is not the same thing as innocent ignorance) whether one is male or female, parent or child. And hysteria, too, is the impossibility of knowing whether one is male or female. All homosexuals are more or less hysterical, in fact they share with women a deep identity disorder; or, to be more accurate, they have a confused identity.

Only the phallus dispenses identity; any social use of the anus, apart from its sublimated use, creates the risk of a loss of identity. Seen from behind we are all women; the anus does not practise sexual discrimination. The relation between homosexuality and sexual identity is discussed by Ralph R. Greenson,[67] who starts by recording the fact (which he apparently finds surprising) that when homosexuality comes into the conversation, "patients react then with a feeling of anxiety and generally behave as though I had told them they were homosexual!" We already know that it is impossible to speak innocently of homosexuality, and the patient's neurosis therefore begins in the doctor's paranoia. But what is even more striking is that the "patient" (a word which clearly refers to his supposed passivity) should feel this idea to be incriminating and terrifying:

> "If we then proceed with the analysis, the patient will soon describe the feeling of losing a part of himself, some essential though established part, something to do with his sexual identity, with his own answer to the question: who am I? One of my patients expressed this very concisely by saying: 'I have the feeling that you are going to tell me I am neither a man nor a woman, but some kind of monster'."[68]

The writer distinguishes three stages in the child's "progress" to adulthood:

> "I am myself, John
> I am myself, John, a boy
> I am myself, John a boy, now with the desire to have sexual activity with girls."[69]

The difference in the sexes and the attraction exercised by one sex upon the other are the preconditions of sexual identity:

87

"The least sexual attraction (of the patient) to a man could throw him into a state of deep panic and endanger his sexual identity."[70]

Let us set aside for the moment the question of the relation between sexual drive and sexual object. The fact remains that the basic precondition of one's sexual identity is the dual certainty of similarity and difference, of narcissism and heterosexuality.

The phallic stage is the identity stage. If you are a boy, you will have relationships with girls. As for your anus, keep it strictly to yourself. Sexual identity is either the certainty of belonging to the master race or the fear of being excluded from it. Someone like Aschenbach, in *Death in Venice,* knows his ancestors:

"What would they have said? What, indeed, would they have said to his entire life, that varied to the point of degeneracy from theirs?"[71]

If the writer is constantly reminded of his past greatness, it is in fact because he feels it slipping away from him, disappearing down to his very name, as his obsession with Tadzio grows stronger. His own appearance becomes so detached from him that even the worst kind of make-up can now give him illusions: in the barber's shop, with his dyed hair, his lipstick and his powdered face, he becomes aware of the fragility of this identity. At first Aschenbach felt the conflict between high and low, between his drive and his stern, distinguished image, but:

"In his very soul he tasted the bestial degradation of his fall. The unhappy man woke from his dream shattered, unhinged, powerless in the demon's grip. He no longer avoided men's eyes nor cared whether he exposed himself to suspicion."[72]

Aschenbach's great surrender is his discovery of the lure of the imaginary, as the incomprehensible homosexual desire takes over.

Young Törless's perplexities come from his inability to picture his desire for Basini in an anthropomorphic, humanly acceptable form; at the moment of his first experience with his fellow-student, Törless cries to himself, "This is not myself! It's not

me! . . . But tomorrow it will be me again! . . . Tomorrow."
And in the remarkable passage where the headmaster, the chaplain and the maths master strive to find a meaning in Törless's delirium, what they are actually trying to do is restore his consciousness of guilt.

It is no longer I who am speaking when the desiring use of the anus asserts itself. The problem here is not one of activity or passivity (which, according to Freud, become differentiated precisely at the anal stage). Homosexuality is always connected with the anus, even though — as Kinsey's precious statistics demonstrate — anal intercourse is still the exception even among homosexuals.

All homosexuality is concerned with anal eroticism, whatever the differentiations and perverse re-territorialisations to which the Oedipus complex subsequently subjects it. The anus is not a substitute for the vagina : women have one as well as men. The phallus's signifying-discerning function is established at the very same moment that the anus-organ breaks away from its imposed privatisation, in order to take part in the desire race. To reinvest the anus collectively and libidinally would involve a proportional weakening of the great phallic signifier, which dominates us constantly both in the small-scale hierarchies of the family and in the great social hierarchies. The least acceptable desiring operation (precisely because it is the most desublimating one) is that which is directed at the anus.

The competitive society and the rule of the phallus

Ours is a competitive society : competition between males, between phallus bearers. The anus is excluded from the social field, and the individuals created by the rule of the bourgeoisie believe that everything revolves around the possession of the phallus, the seizure of other people's phalluses or the fear of losing one's own. Freud's reconstruction merely translates and internalises this pitiless rule of the competitive hierarchy. You build better by castrating others; you can only ascend to genitality by trampling over other phallus bearers on the way. You are a phallus bearer only if you are recognised as such by others. Your phallus is constantly threatened : you are in constant fear of losing a phallus

89

which was difficult to win in the first place. No one ever threatens to take away your anus. There is more of a threat in someone disclosing that you too have an anus, that it can be used. Schreber both fears and desires to be raped by Flechsig; his fear arises because the disclosure that he is also an anus challenges his phallic existence.

The relation of man the phallus bearer to other men can only take place under the rule of competition for a single possible object of sexual activity, woman. Competition "begins" in the family, with the father and the brothers. It "continues" throughout the social process, as it ascends the hierarchy. To own or not to own, to possess a woman or not to possess her; that is the problem which the world around us poses, the "apparent" problem which conceals desiring production.

Psychoanalysts admit that all normal people are more or less paranoid. The relations of property and possession institute the system of jealousy in the form of society's generalised paranoia. We have already seen how Freud established the relation between paranoia and the self-suppression of homosexuality. In a 1922 paper he distinguishes between a *competitive* jealousy, which he calls "normal", a *projected* jealousy which goes with resistance to transgressions (such as adultery) tolerated by society, and a *delusional* jealousy of a paranoiac nature. The only purpose of making such distinctions is to reassure the reader that there are some differentiations, quantitative ones at least, between the normal and the pathological. Indeed, the first type of jealousy is the result of "grief about the man, whom he loves unconsciously, and hatred of the woman as his rival";[73] Freud knew of a jealous man whose "sense of helplessness" and "the images he used to describe his condition . . . were referred by him to impressions received during several homosexual acts of aggression to which he had been subjected as a boy".[74] And projected jealousy, which society in its wisdom gives rise to by admitting that a certain element of infidelity in marriage is inevitable, "has . . . an almost delusional character".[75] But it is the analysis of delusional jealousy itself that shows why Freud felt obliged to tone down his discovery with these little embellishments. It was unthinkable for Freud to make a frontal and unannounced attack on the jealousy-competition system.

"Delusional jealousy is what is left of a homosexuality that has run its course. . . . As an attempt at defence against an unduly strong homosexual impulse it may, in a man, be described in the formula : '*I* do not love him, *she* loves him!' "[76] In other words : I cannot love him, since it is she whom I love and who loves him.

Persecutory delusion is the reconstruction of an imaginary that will enable the subject to defend himself against the emergence of homosexual desire. "We know that with the paranoiac it is precisely the most loved person of his own sex that becomes his persecutor."[77] The jealousy-competition system is opposed to the system of non-exclusive desire, and puts up an increasing number of defensive barriers against it. With regard to relations among men, "the behaviour towards men in general of a man who sees in other men potential love-objects must be different from that of a man who looks upon other men in the first instance as rivals in regard to women."[78] The jealousy-competition system is primitively opposed to the polyvocal system of desire. Homosexual desire also has something of this opposition, but its social use takes the sublimated form of a devotion to "men in general" and the public interest, to use Freud's language. Thus the sublimation of homosexuality can be seen as a public utility. The ambiguity arises with the vagueness of Freud's terms, "social instinctual impulses . . . devotion to the interests of the community,"[79] etc. This alleged social sense constitutes precisely the exploitation of homosexual desire and its transformation into a force for social cohesion, the component and necessary counterpart of a jealousy-competition system which, if pushed to its limit, would be an absolute law of the jungle.

Homosexual sublimation provides the solid ideological basis for a constantly threatened social unity. Capitalist society can only organise its relationships around the jealousy-competition system by means of the dual action of repression and sublimation of homosexuality; one underwrites the competitive rule of the phallus, the other the hypocrisy of human relationships. The phallocratic competitive society is based on the repression of desires directed at the anus; the repression of homosexuality is directly related to the jealousy paranoia that constitutes the daily fabric of society, and to the ideology of an integral social

91

whole, the "human community" we live in.

Homosexual love is not free from rivalry and jealousy; in exchange for services rendered by the transformation of the homosexual libido, the competition-jealousy system dresses up as homosexual love. This it does so well that some people credit homosexual desire iteslf with originating the jealous paranoia for which it is in fact compelled to serve as a driving force : in the terms of Stekel's psychological analysis, jealousy is related to homosexuality because the latter is actually a means of representing to oneself the rival's phallus. If men are in competition with each other, then the sexual relation between men (and here, of course, he forgets to specify that this is repressed and exclusively imaginary) is a relation between phalluses, a comparative and hierarchical relation. Homosexuality thus becomes phallic, in exchange for permitting the repression of desires directed at the anus and thus enabling the phallus to triumph. The release of homosexual desire from the system of the imaginary in which it is exploited has therefore become essential to the destruction of the jealousy-competition system.

Oedipal reproduction and homosexuality

Homosexual desire is related in particular to the pre-personal state of desire. To this is linked the fear of loss of identity, as it is state of desire. To this is linked the fear of identity, as it is experienced by the imaginary in the repressed state. The direct manifestation of homosexual desire stands in contrast to the relations of identity, the necessary roles imposed by the Oedipus complex in order to ensure the reproduction of society. Reproductive sexuality is also the reproduction of the Oedipus complex; family heterosexuality guarantees not only the production of children but also (and chiefly) Oedipal reproduction, with its differentiation between parents and children. In 1909 Freud wrote a paper entitled "Family Romances", which is the article of faith of Oedipal reproduction :

> "For a small child his parents are at first the only authority and the source of all belief. The child's most intense and most momentous wish during these early years is to be like

92

his parents (that is, the parent of his own sex) and to be big like his father and mother."[80]

By becoming a father in turn, the former child hands the Oedipus complex down to his own descendants like the torch of civilisation, and takes his place in the great lineage of Humanity. The absolute need for the Oedipus complex to be reproduced — and not produced — explains why childhood conflicts with the father image are finally resolved by the son's stepping into his father's shoes and founding a new family: "indeed, the whole progress of society rests on the opposition between successive generations."[81] This is how the game of taboo and transgression is historically transmitted. However, Freud adds:

"On the other hand, there is a class of neurotics whose condition is recognisably determined by their having failed in this task."[82]

Their state is conditioned: they must be fully conscious of having failed the historical task assigned to them, so that the social significance of that task may not be weakened. To reduce the revolt of the young to the level of a "generation gap" means to impose a choice dictated by the rule of the double-bind: do as your parents did, or be neurotic. The May 1968 movement in France, for example, was plagued by the need to make a choice imposed by the dominant ideology: either be a responsible politician, or a neurotic individual.

Homosexual neurosis is the backlash to the threat which homosexual desire poses for Oedipal reproduction. Homosexual desire is the ungenerating-ungenerated terror of the family, because it produces itself without reproducing. Every homosexual must thus see himself as the end of the species, the termination of a process for which he is not responsible and which must stop at himself. The homosexual is possible socially only if he has a neurotic "fixation" to his mother or father; he is the by-product of a line which is finished and which turns his guilt at existing only in relation to the past into the very meaning of his perversion. The homosexual can only be a degenerate, for he does not generate — he is only the artistic end to a species. The only acceptable form of homosexual temporality is that which

93

is directed towards the past, to the Greeks or Sodom; as long as homosexuality serves no purpose, it may at least be allowed to contribute that little non-utilitarian "something" towards the upkeep of the artistic spirit. Homosexuality is seen as a regressive neurosis, totally drawn towards the past; the homosexual is incapable of facing his future as an adult and father, which is laid down for every male individual. Since homosexual desire is ignorant of the law of succession — the law of stages — and is thus unable to ascend to genitality, it must therefore be regression, a counter-current to the necessary historical evolution, like an eddy on the surface of a river. Freud undoubtedly establishes a topographical coexistence of drives rather than successive stages; but temporality asserts itself as the absolute need for parents and children to succeed each other, and for full genitality to follow the anal stage, even if the preceding stages reappear throughout the individual's history as the relics of an everthreatening past. The counter-current is merely the gratuitous little flourish that responds to the inevitability of the current.

Homosexuals have their own way of dealing with the law of inevitable ageing, of Oedipal temporality. From under the rouge and the cosmetics, Aschenbach sees in the mirror an adolescent in full bloom in his own image, with his mythical youth restored. Homosexual desire is unaware of the passing of the seven ages of man, and homosexuals therefore experience all the more intensely, and in a greater concentration of images than anyone else, the Oedipal trap of an evolution from infancy to old age.

In psychoanalysis, everything begins with the child; but at the same time, the child only exists through the Oedipal projection of the father's paranoia. According to the authors of *L'Anti-Oedipe* :

> "From the point of view of regression, which has only a *hypothetical* sense, the father comes before the child. . . . Guilt is an idea projected by the father before becoming an internal feeling experienced by the son. . . . If regression taken in the absolute proves inadequate, it is because it encloses us in simple reproduction or generation."[83]

The psychoanalytical point of view is one of temporal succession, of guilt handed down along the line. According to this view,

94

the homosexual is a neurotic product of his parents' paranoia; because homosexual desire to some extent reveals the process of the self-production of desire, there is a special need to construct a temporality for it. Homosexuality is regressive because it is the form which Oedipalisation attributes to homosexual desire as an expression of the libido's temporal (and unacceptable) ignorance.

Homosexuality is regressive because otherwise the homosexual would be both an orphan and childless. He would be an orphan in the sense of Deleuze and Guattari's statement, "The unconscious is an orphan". And he would be childless in the sense that the transmission of homosexuality has something faintly mysterious about it, like the production of desire: a Prefect of Police quoted by Gustave Macé defines homosexuals as "people who, though not procreating, have a marked tendency to multiply."[84] Homosexual production takes place according to a mode of non-limitative horizontal relations, heterosexual reproduction according to one of hierarchical succession. In the Oedipal system, every individual knows that it will one day be his turn to occupy the place already determined by the triangle; according to Freud, this is one of the preconditions of society's progress. Deleuze and Guattari explain that alongside the male-female disjunction which is the constant outcome of filiation, male homosexuality, far from being a product of the Oedipus complex, constitutes a totally different mode of social relation; they are therefore demonstrating that besides the Freudian myth which derives everything from filiation,[85] there is another possible social relation which is not vertical but horizontal.

On the one hand, in so far as he represents the possibility of that repressed relation, the non-sublimated homosexual is a social misfit in the heterosexual family society; Adler (in the above-mentioned work) writes that "the homosexual does not seek a peaceful and harmonious adjustment to society, and his effusive inclination . . . leads him along a path of ceaseless struggle. . . . In short, the homosexual has not developed into a partner of human society."[86] Here, "human society" means of course the Freudian model, in which homosexuality can only find a place according to the sublimated Oedipal mode.

On the other hand, the homosexual points the way to another possible form of relationship which we hardly dare call "society".

Homosexual grouping

Sublimated homosexuality provides society with the minimum of humanitarian cohesion it needs. The repression of homosexuality corresponds to the jealousy-competition system of the phallic individual. Freud wrote in 1922 :

> "In the light of psychoanalysis we are accustomed to regard social feeling as a sublimation of homosexual attitudes towards objects."[87]

It would be interesting to try and describe what "social" relations not based on homosexual sublimation might be like, or, alternatively, to envisage what effects the desublimation of homosexuality would have on social organisation. Freud concludes his essay with an ambiguous remark :

> "In the homosexuals with marked social interests, it would seem that the detachment of social feeling from object-choice has not been fully carried through."[88]

This remark is particularly unsatisfactory, from the Freudian point of view : the idea is that the amount of social interests should proportionally reduce the amount of libido directed towards the homosexual object. But in this "homosexual with marked social interests" we come up against a monster of contradictions, unless we take the word "social' to indicate something other than what it usually implies. If the direct expression of homosexual desire were to take a social direction, it would certainly not be in this society, which is based on the domination of anti-homosexual paranoia and sublimation in the form of the heterosexual family system.

The desires directed towards the anus, which are closely connected with homosexual desire, constitute what we shall call a "group" mode of relations as opposed to the usual "social" mode. The anus undergoes the movement of privatisation; the publicising or, to be more precise, the desiring "grouping" [*groupalisation*] of the anus, would cause the collapse of both the sublimating phallic hierarchy and the individual/society double-bind.

Deleuze and Guattari explain that no individual phantasy can be opposed to the collective phantasy, or in other words that the individual himself is a kind of collective phantasy, the fruit of a collectivity based on Oedipal oppression. To deal with homosexuality as an individual problem, as *the* individual problem, is the surest way to subject it to the Oedipus complex. Homosexual desire is a group desire; it groups the anus by restoring its functions as a desiring bond, and by collectively reinvesting it against a society which has reduced it to the state of a shameful little secret. "Practising" homosexuals are, in a sense, people who have failed their sublimation; they are "incapable of fully assuming the demands which nature and culture may impose on individuals".[89]

To fail one's sublimation is in fact merely to conceive social relations in a different way. Possibly, when the anus recovers its desiring function and the plugging in of organs takes place subject to no rule or law, the group can then take its pleasure in an immediate relation where the sacrosanct difference between public and private, between the individual and the social, will be out of place. We can find traces of this state of primary sexual communism in some of the institutions of the homosexual ghetto, despite all the repressions and guilty reconstructions which these undergo: in Turkish baths, for example, where homosexual desires are plugged in anonymously, in spite of ever-present fears that the police may be present. The grouping of the anus is not open to sublimation, it offers not the slightest crack for the guilty conscience to infiltrate.

The anus's group mode is an annular one, a circle which is open to an infinity of directions and possibilities for plugging in, with no set places. The group annular mode (one is tempted to spell it "anular") causes the "social" of the phallic hierarchy, the whole house of cards of the "imaginary", to collapse.

Homosexual desire is not some secondary consequence of the Oedipus complex: it is the operation of a desiring machine plugged into the anus. Deleuze and Guattari point to the mistakes of writers, such as Devereux,[90] who see homosexuality as the product of Oedipal repression. We shall see further on, when we come to the question of masochism, why this "secondariness" is attributed to certain manifestations of desire. Deleuze and Guattari insist on the following:

"If it is true that there is an Oedipal or filiative homosexuality, we must see it merely as a secondary reaction to group homosexuality, which is never Oedipal."[91]

Thus homosexual desire exists only in the group, yet at the same time is banned from society. Hence the need to eliminate the anal, or rather to transform it into anality. Freud writes:

"The first prohibition which a child comes across — the prohibition against getting pleasure from anal activity and its products — has a decisive effect on his whole development. This must be the first occasion on which the infant has a glimpse of an environment hostile to his instinctual impulses, on which he learns to separate his own entity from this alien one and on which he carries out the first 'repression' of his possibilities for pleasure. From that time on, what is 'anal' remains the symbol of everything that is to be repudiated and excluded from life."[92]

Freud explains in his *Introductory Lectures on Psychoanalysis* that anal excitement must be renounced because "everything that has to do with these functions is improper and must be kept secret. (The child) must forgo these sources of pleasure, in the name of social respectability."[93]

Homosexual desire becomes homosexuality and falls into the trap of the Oedipus complex because the anal "group" is a threat to the Oedipal "social". The Oedipus myth enables us to understand the need to distinguish between homosexual desire, a primary homosexuality which reveals the lack of differentiation of desire, and a perverse Oedipal homosexuality, all of whose energy goes into reinforcing the Law. In the words of Deleuze and Guattari, "Everything begins in the mind of Laius, that old group homosexual, that pervert who sets a trap for desire." Oedipal homosexuality begins in the father's head, and guarantees that the group energy will be integrated into the Oedipal social structure.

98

5

HOMOSEXUAL "OBJECT-CHOICE" AND HOMOSEXUAL "BEHAVIOUR"

The neurotic family romance turns homosexual desire into neurotic homosexuality; hence the manufacture of a "psychological history" for the homosexual, together with its corresponding "behaviour'. Everyone seems to be welcome at the tavern of homosexuality: sociologists are free to sit down with psychiatrists. One cannot say that there is no such thing as homosexual behaviour, but all the word "behaviour" indicates is a sum total of categorisations and restrictions on a sexual activity that tends to break free; the reality of a homosexual behaviour with its own constants is as impossible to determine as the Oedipus complex from which it springs. The sociologist blithely locates the unconscious among the great molar social machines; to him it is a truly civilised unconscious, and the unfathomable depths of homosexuality appear, like incest, to be "a shallow, misrepresented stream".

There is no homosexual "choice", since the choice can only be experienced through the effort to discover (in Genêt's words) "enough reasons to be called by such a name". At most we can speak of a homosexual outlet, a deceptively clear path which homosexual desire is forced to take in order to survive. This is Sartre's description of the process:

> "Inversion is not the result of a prenatal choice, nor of a glandular malformation, nor is it even the passive and determinate result of complexes: it is a way out such as the child discovers when he is about to suffocate."[94]

And the child is not yet aware that the air he gulps at is poisoned, that what is offered to him is but the inversion, the *recto* of the normality to which he is bound. Genêt's case history is instructive. It is significant that Sartre calls him a "saint": to take one's pleasure outside the system becomes, with the transcendental intervention of the Oedipus complex, a "will to evil", an existential choice which Sartre is so kind as to describe for us step-by-step. In his version, a metaphysical freedom to opt for homosexual sterility replaces the productive functioning of the libido. In the eyes of the progressive intelligentsia, the "will to evil" sanctifies everything that is intolerable about desire and thus preserves it.

Undoubtedly Sartre is partly right, inasmuch as he is describing the reality of a particular imaginary. But what is this "suffocation" which the child escapes? Is it the impending threat of sexual normalisation? In this case, the homosexual outlet is the only way of living with one's desiring function, whatever the social consequences may be. But could it not also be the child's fear of losing his ego if the possibilities for the plugging in of desire are not reinterpreted in terms of responsibility and guilt?

As Hercules stood between vice and virtue, he must surely have felt the rule of the "double-bind'. Two roads, no more. To represent the homosexual choice in such terms means reducing it to the framework from which it is trying to escape. Homosexual desire is in fact a desire for pleasure whatever the system, and not merely inside or outside the system. Sade's Justine and Juliette choose two different paths: one which society calls the virtuous path, the other which it sees as the road to vice. However, the symmetry is only apparent: Justine's virtuous choice turns her into a libertine against her will, a neurotic who constantly wallows in the guilt caused by the dissolute way of life into which she has been plunged. Juliette, rather than choosing, refuses to eliminate anything; she believes that everything is possible, that she can draw pleasure from every situation and that ultimately all the ways of plugging in desire are good.

In fact the homosexual "choice" is only a rationalisation operated by the Oedipal system, by means of a differentiation among whole people in a relation of exclusive object-choice.

The "object-choice"

The homosexual "outlet" is characterised by the choice of an object of the same sex as oneself. "Self", "object", "same" are all anthropomorphic characterisations of desire. They pre-

100

suppose the differentiation between the ego and the outside world, the construction of a subject capable of operating on the lines of the "similar" and the "different":

"Object-choice, the step forward in the development of the libido which is made after the narcissistic stage, can take place according to two different types: either according to the *narcissistic type,* where the subject's own ego is replaced by another one that is as similar as possible, or according to the *anaclitic type,* where people who have become indispensable because they guarantee the satisfaction of other vital needs are chosen as objects of the libido. A strong libidinal fixation to the narcissistic type of object-choice is part of the predisposition to manifest homosexuality."[95]

We have already come across this knot of narcissism. The inevitable complement of the operation of turning the libidinal energy back on to itself is a system of "object-choice" that conforms to the norms of similarity and difference.

Freud gives the following account in *Three Essays on the Theory of Sexuality*:

"The sexual instinct* and sexual object are merely soldered together — a fact which we have been in danger of overlooking in consequence of the uniformity of the normal picture, where the object appears to form part and parcel of the instinct. . . . It seems probable that the sexual instinct is in the first instance independent of its object."[96]

It is in fact precisely to the homosexual drive* that such a statement can be applied. Freud's study of "perversion" demonstrates that the connection between the drive and the object (either man or woman) is "self-evident" only because there is a social ideology which gives sexuality its form. Perversions, and homosexuality in particular, point to what remains hidden in normal sexuality.

---

* The modern English translation ("drive") of Freud's concept of *Trieb* is preferred here; however the original translation ("instinct") has been maintained in quotations from the standard edition. For a discussion of this problem, see Laplanche and Pontalis, *The Language of Psychoanalysis*.

The opposition between perversions and normal sexuality under-lines the arbitrary nature of the bridge between object-choice and behaviour as a whole. Reproductive family heterosexuality considers the sexual attraction between man and woman (as the sexual objects) to be self-evident, so that in a sense there appears to be no difference between the sexual drive and its object. Freud regards the emergence of an apparently deviant object-choice as the illuminating crack through which homosexual desire manifests its incapability of being reduced to a definite object-choice. The homosexual "perversion" manifests this lack of differentiation inasmuch as its object-choice is not self-evident; but it also testifies to the power of the normalising forces at work, inasmuch as it seems — admittedly in its own way and its own time — to obey the rule which connects a given object-choice to a given behaviour. The representation of sexuality as a sexual drive attracted by a sort of chemistry to its complement, i.e. the natural (or perverse) sexual object of this drive, enables psycho-logical personalities to be constituted according to the classic characterisations which demarcate desire along arbitrary lines. To enable the term "sexual drive" to directly express a harmon-ious whole converging on a given sexual object, for "object" read "persons", so that the sexual drive may in turn embody other recognisable psychological persons.

Freud's thought becomes oedipalised at the point when poly-vocal, non-personalised relations among organs change into relations between whole people who represent the reality of the first relations among organs. In Freud, the component drive always functions independently; "each strives on its own account, for the satisfaction of its own desires". However, from childhood we gradually tend to interpret the component drive's relationship to its component object (breast, penis) as a relationship to the whole person, and in particular to the mother. For example Muldworf, the communist party's theoretician, goes so far as to uphold the myth of a "fusion" during which infant and mother are one, thus endowing the drive with a tendency towards the psychological formation of the person. The component nature of the instinct and the term "component object" are subject to the same problems as the term "perverse", which is used in connec-tion with the polymorphism of desire.[97]

And yet on the question of the sexual object, Freud is sufficiently explicit about what is to be understood by the differentiation between normal and deviant, and consequently between the component and the whole. "Deviation in respect of the sexual object" is to be understood as a "deviation in respect of the sexual aim", which is tied to genitality.[98] Deviations concern other erotogenic zones than the genital one, they are a universal phenomenon, and (this is where the ambiguity of Freud's reasoning lies) are essential to the formation of the "normal", this latter being the inevitable climax of a sexual evolution in which the deviations themselves are stages:

> "We must regard each individual as possessing an anal erotism, a urethral erotism, an oral erotism, etc., and that the existence of mental complexes corresponding to these implies no judgement of abnormality or neurosis."[99]

In other words, desire is at first a universally distributed set of diverse and non-exclusive drives, of erotisms based on the plugging in of organs according to the "and/and" rather than the "either/or" mode.

In order to go from an inclusive system to an exclusive system, in which one choice precludes another, one must first go through the personal characterisation of drives attached to a particular object; reduction of the object-choice to a matter of behaviour enables us to make the division between "good and bad" choices, "good and bad" objects, heterosexuality and homosexuality. The choice then becomes the responsibility of whole persons, in a system which correlates types of behaviour with objects and homosexuality with the choice of persons of the same sex. The heterosexual object-choice becomes the symbol of adult sexuality, under the sign of the genital zone. Freud continues to assert the persistence of a partial component of sexuality, but it now takes the form of regression to a preceding fixation of the libido, and the homosexual object-choice is related to the spread of narcissism and to the importance attached to the anal zone. It is true that in *Three Essays* Freud insists on the difference between our modern erotic life, which favours the object and attributes to it a sense of guilt or non-guilt, and the erotic life of the ancients, which emphasised Eros, the drive itself:

"The ancients glorified the instinct and were prepared on its account to honour even an inferior object; while we despise the instinctual activity in itself, and find excuses for it only in the merits of the object."[100]

This comparison shows Freud's awareness of the fact that in our society the sexual act is not considered as production, but as a vacuum to be filled by the full sexual object. These socially appointed objects enable the indifferentiation of desire to be eliminated; they are modern society's ways of telling desire that caresses must be controlled, that they must follow the course marked out by the established relation between the drive and the sexual object, in its normal form and therefore also in its perverse form. The comparison between normalcy and perversion is an ambiguous one, since it constructs a sexual history with a regressive antiquity, precisely in order to exclude it.

The homosexual perversion must submit to the rule which assigns certain objects to certain drives in an exclusive way, just as it must submit to the rule of fixation to the parental person : these bonds are needed to stop the drift of desire. The strictly fixed object-choice is an insurance against the decentering which both the phallus and genitality would then suffer. We all know that homosexual caresses have a greater tendency to stray over all the zones of the body than heterosexual caresses, whose aim is clearly determined. The relative imprecision of aim in homosexual activity allows for numerous forms, from fellatio to sodomy. With homosexuality, therefore, it is particularly important to give a direction to the choices and to inject them with feelings of guilt about their objects. The triple equivalence "choice = exclusive choice = personality" encounters some difficulties with homosexuality, but eventually succeeds in establishing homosexual perversion as a behaviour based on apparently natural certainties.

Freud himself criticised the naïveté of those who think it possible to infer behaviour from object-choice where homosexuality is concerned. Experience has proved the thesis that effeminate men are attracted to masculine ones and vice-versa to be quite absurd. The categorisation of so-called passive sodomy as "effeminate" is not even based on the material reality of homosexual relationships, where men who are considered most

104

masculine are surely not necessarily, nor even in the majority of cases, the "male" partners.

Similarly, homosexual effeminacy is not necessarily related to the choice of the penis as the favourite pleasure object. Sartre's description of fellatio as the demasculinisation of the male — he sees it as a kind of castration — is a clear indication that in this field things are certainly not as simple as the comfortable cushion of natural certainties ("queers love big virile organs") would have us believe.

The beginning of Proust's *Sodom and Gomorrah* contains the most clearcut example of how homosexual perversion in relation to the object-choice may be constituted. The heterosexual object-choice is easy and natural, the sexual drive seeming to imply it as self-evident. The homosexual object-choice is perverse in so far as it seeks difficulty :

> "Lovers from whom is always precluded the possibility of that love the hope of which gives them the strength to endure so many risks and so much loneliness, since they fall in love with precisely that type of man who has nothing feminine about him, who is not an invert and consequently cannot love them in return; with the result that their desire would be for ever insatiable did not their money procure for them real men, and their imagination end by making them take for real men the inverts to whom they had prostituted themselves."[101]

The confusion between the object-choice and the subject's sexual nature, wich Freud attacks in "The Psychogenesis of a Case of Female Homosexuality", applies not only to "normality" but also to homosexuality. In the latter case it operates in the perverse form of a drive which has great difficulty in finding its natural object and which thereby has the appeal of being almost impossible. Homosexuals love heterosexual men and heterosexual men love women. The tragedy is well constructed : homosexual love is torn between an inescapable object-choice and the impossibility of fulfilling it. The perversity of homosexual desire is rooted in the fact that it constitutes the caricature or negative of the heterosexual object-choice; it acts as a feedback to the latter, as if testifying to the strength of the connection between

105

sexual drive and sexual object. The sophism of the "accursed race", and of homosexual perversion as a whole, lies in the fact that the word "virile" describes anyone who is not "queer", while the "queer" is the penis lover, and the penis is the phallus, i.e. the organ of virility; and so the circle of impossible loves is closed.

The primacy of genitality emerges strengthened from this double relation, in which the pervert acknowledges the normal person as the impossible object of his desire. The one-time Freudian, Alfred Adler, pushed this primacy to its extreme. He developed the theme of "virile protest", saying that sexual phenomena and their consequences are determined by the existence of the individual's general tendency to refuse the "feminine line", in order to reach or remain on the masculine line. Adler's whole characterology is derived from this idea of "virile protest". It is a sociological translation of the great phallic signifier, dividing human beings into people who are afraid of losing their penis and people who wish they had one.

In fact, to centre the homosexual drive on the wish to appropriate the penis of others is the same as deriving it from castration anxiety. Sex is reduced to the penis, this being the homosexual's only possible sexual "object", whereas the woman remains the only possible *social* sexual "object" (as a whole person). Thus the homosexual somehow becomes a subject who dreams of being an object, in his mad desire for the one and only component object, the penis; homosexuality thus seems to be content to take over the given elements of normal sexuality, merely changing their sign. To centre on the penis eliminates or subdues the other desiring machines, by means of the creation of a closed and univocal object-person.

The soldering together of behaviour and choice is expressed in this case by the transformation of the homosexual into a substitute woman, through his attempt to constitute himself as an object of heterosexual desire when he is actually its "natural" subject. The fact that an effeminate man may not necessarily be "female" in the sexual act does not affect this arbitrary but solid construction. The homosexual is an artificial woman, the image of an image, since the woman herself is constituted as the sole sexual object only through the play of the imaginary.

The "third sex" and "masculine-feminine"

The world is divided into subject and object, male and female. Man desires woman, the woman's desire is of no consequence. In order to classify the homosexual, we must pass through the system of the similar or the different, i.e. the similar *and* the different. The homosexual is both different (the third sex) and similar (he subdivides into male and female). The discourse on homosexuality is locked permanently inside the cage of these two possibilities.

The homosexual *ought* to be different, otherwise every one would be homosexual. And despite Freud's struggle against the third sex theory, it keeps reappearing in various forms. "Congenital homosexuality" hasn't lost its appeal: the chromosome theory, for example, reconciles the similar and the different by differentiating between a small minority of people who are "racially" homosexual (because they possess one chromosome too many) and a majority of homosexuals who are such "by culture", which can be explained by the individual's psychological history. The difference must be reduced to a similarity, because no normal individual would admit to being a homosexual; but homosexuals must not take advantage of this by thinking they can be free of phallic and Oedipal predominance. This is why Hirschfeld's attempt to organise the liberation of homosexuals on the basis of the innate and irrepressible nature of their tastes was doomed to failure.

Such a theory certainly has the advantage of allowing the dominant ideology to cast the male homosexual in a role which safeguards the discriminating value of the penis, without which one could simply cast him as a woman. But short of putting all homosexuals into concentration camps, it arouses the danger of letting more than two sexes coexist side by side, of giving up the simple binary system. If there are three sexes, why not more? When it is not totally fascist, the third sex theory is dangerous. Freud fought against this theory in the interests of homosexuals themselves. Everyone is more or less homosexual; there is no reason to see homosexuals as a separate category. But beneath this universalisation of homosexuality in fact lurks the universalisation of the Oedipus complex. Oedipal imperialism finds it particularly useful to show that beneath the difference lies the similarity; it is particularly reassuring to normal sexuality for the same categories to appear in both homosexuals and heterosexuals, thus stressing the undeniable universality of the phallic signifier. It is, therefore, useful both for the homosexual to be different and for his difference to be reduced to a similarity; it is essential that he be different yet subject to the same rules.

Criticising the third sex theory, Freud wrote that "[this group of] perverts . . . seeks to achieve very much the same ends with the objects of their desires as normal people do with theirs."[102] Homosexuals have simply chosen the wrong object. We can then subdivide them into males and females, and reassert in their terms the universality of the law which binds the sexual drive to its object, a law which they caricature. We can call this the heterosexual conception of the homosexual world : in repressing the other drives, the heterosexual drive channels them through its own order of things. How do people of the same sex practise a sexuality which is defined by the relation between two different sexes? By a simple game of substitution, in which the fundamental law of heterosexuality reappears.

However, homosexuality could upset the clarity of this kind of functional subdivision between subject and object, male and female. The whole issue of the debate regularly raised by psychiatrists (see p. 87) as to whether homosexuality is a perversion or, on the contrary, several different phenomena arbitrarily grouped together under this heading, becomes clear in the light of this double need to divide and rule by maintaining the perverse difference. Ferenczi elevated this combinatorial faculty of the sexes as applied to homosexuality to its highest degree. In "The Nosology of Male Homosexuality (Homo-Erotism)", he made a now classic division of homosexuality into masculine and feminine :

> "It seemed to me from the beginning that the designation 'homosexuality' was nowadays applied to dissimilar and unrelated psychical abnormalities. Sexual relations with members of one's own sex are only a symptom . . ."[103]

Freud had written :

> "What we have thrown together, for reasons of convenience,

108

under the name of homosexuality may derive from a diversity of processes of psychosexual inhibition and the process which we have uncovered may only be one among many others, and related to one given type of homosexuality."[104]

Homosexuals were alas unable to enjoy their acknowledged diversity for long, for it led to a new classification. Ferenczi insisted on a sharp distinction between "subject homo-erotism" and "object homo-erotism" :

"A man who in intercourse with men feels himself to be a woman is inverted in respect to his own ego (homo-erotism through subject-inversion, or, more shortly, 'subject homo-erotism'); he feels himself to be a woman, and this not only in genital intercourse, but in all relations of life."[105]

In contrast to this passive homosexual there must obviously be a masculine, active homosexual :

"He feels himself a man in every respect, is as a rule very energetic and active, and there is nothing effeminate to be discovered in his bodily or mental organisation. The object of his inclination alone is unchanged, so that one might call him a homo-erotic through exchange of the love-object, or, more shortly, an object homo-erotic."[106]

The characterology thus firmly binds the sexual drive to its object : the subject homo-erotic is attracted to masculine and mature men, the object homo-erotic to delicate young boys. Krafft-Ebing had already postulated the existence of two nervous centres in the individual, one male, the other female. The common definition of the homosexual as "a feminine brain in a masculine body"[107] is complemented here by a detailed characterology. Ferenczi indicated that he was aware that the qualifying adjectives of "feminine" and "masculine" which he applied to the invert and to the homo-erotic were purely ideological. But he filled in the picture in these terms :

"It may be . . . indicated here that by *maleness* I understand *activity* (aggressivity) of the sexual hunger, highly developed object-love with overestimation of the object, a polygamy that is in only apparent contrast with the latter trait, and, as a distant derivative of the activity, intellectual talent; by *femaleness* I understand *passivity* (tendency to repression), narcissism and intuitiveness. The physical attributes of sex are, of course, mingled in every individual — although in unequal proportion."[108]

In other words, it is all just a matter of the dosage — but the general characteristics are permanent. We have here one of the best descriptions of the dominant sexual ideology and of the values attached to it, and chance has it that it was written about homosexuality.

Sartre's book *Saint-Genêt* is at times the faithful reflection of this discourse :

"The priority, in the subject itself, of the object over the subject can lead to passivity in love and this, when it affects a male, can incline him towards homosexuality."[109]

The invert or subject homo-erotic embodies the incurable pervert, upon whom classical psychiatry in particular heaps abuse and shame. Ferenczi stated that "the true invert is hardly ever impelled to seek medical advice, he feels at complete ease in the passive role."[110] He is completely different from men, and resembles women. The maculine or object homo-erotic, on the other hand, is described as follows :

"[He] is uncommonly tormented by the consciousness of his abnormality; sexual intercourse never completely satisfies him, he is tortured by qualms of conscience, and over-estimates his sexual object to the uttermost. That he is plagued with conflicts and never comes to terms with his condition is shown by his repeated attempts to obtain medical help for his trouble."[111]

The object homo-erotic is perfectly similar to men, a curable pervert who is conscious of his guilt. The third sex and the necessary similarity combine : the invert is, according to Ferenczi, "a veritable sexual intermediate, a pure anomaly of development. On the other hand, the object homo-erotic is a neurotic, an obsessional neurotic." Inversion is incurable, object homo-erotism curable. The parallel is only an apparent one; if anything, we should speak of complementarity.

110

Homosexuals are thus subdivided functionally : either they are different from normal people in respect of the object of their desire and similar as subjects, or they are different as subjects but similar in respect of the object. Both the similar and the different therefore operate effectively among them. In *Three Essays on the Theory of Sexuality*, Freud distinguishes between a complete inversion which can be related to the subject homo-erotic, in which the man feels like a woman, and an amphigenic inversion or psychosexual hermaphroditism in which some male functions are preserved.[112] All these subdivisions of homosexuality lead in any case to the restoration, amidst the homosexual confusion, of the subject-object and male-female principles.

The complementarity of the two types of homosexual as analysed by Ferenczi ensures the existence of a microcosmic homosexual world which luckily can be compared point by point with the heterosexual one, is metaphorically related to it as one entity parallel to another, and is cursed with being but a perverse caricature of normality : the males who represent its consciousness are in fact merely neurotics. Ferenczi writes as follows :

"It may happen that two homo-erotics of different types unite to form a pair. The invert finds in the object homo-erotic a quite suitable lover, who adores him, supports him in material affairs, and is imposing and energetic; the man of the objective type, on the other hand, may find pleasure in just the mixture of masculine and feminine traits present in the invert."[113]

The situation thus becomes socially stable, in all its neurotic instability. The homosexual microcosm is a closed one, yet at the same time is incapable of existing on its own; it is threatened with a permanent imbalance in the form of the male's neurosis. Ferenczi hastens to add the following correction :

"I also know homo-erotics, by the way, who exclusively desire non-inverted youths, and only content themselves with inverts in the absence of the former."[114]

We have here the converse of Proust's description. Proust thinks that homosexuals are perpetually in search of true males, and

111

actually deal with false males only because they agree to make love with other men; the object homo-erotic, however, associates with false young boys — he desires the impossible, a young male who will agree to be female for him. This conception of the homosexual world merely reflects the coherence of the hetero-sexual world by a game of substitution which compounds its neurosis.

We could even go so far as to imagine a mirror of the mirror, according to Ferenczi:

"It must be further remarked that many inverts are by no means quite insusceptible to the endearments of the female sex. It is through intercourse with women (i.e. their like) that they dispose of what may be called the homosexual component of their sexuality."[115]

It would be far simpler, however, to see this as a breakdown of the functional division, as a result of the basic lack of differentiation of desire. Simpler — but of course less effective in the construction of an imaginary where men, women and homosexuals all have their place. Similarly, Ferenczi notes that the dreams of object homo-erotics are "very rich in reversals":

"The symptomatic action of making a slip of the tongue or pen in the use of the gender of articles is common. One patient even made up a bisexual number: the number 101 signified, as the context showed, that for him 'backwards and forwards were the same'."[110]

This patient testified to the indifference of desire to functional divisions, if only through symbols. The differentiation between the object and the subject, and between the drive and what it points to (following the rule that "differences become similar, similarities become different"), accounts for the contradictory phenomena which produce a logic of exclusion. Freud notes that the invert is generally almost as attracted to masculinity as he appears to be towards femininity (a taste for make-up, etc.). Freud's remark doesn't make sense in a system which reserves femininity for the object and masculinity for the subject, and vice-versa in the case of the invert. It begins to make sense when we question the notion of difference between object and subject.

112

Musil speaks of Törless's discovery in the following terms:

> "For although Törless did debase himself with Basini, his desire was never satisfied by him; on the contrary, it went growing out beyond Basini, growing out into some new and aimless craving."[117]

And when the headmaster questions Törless in order to put a name to what his behaviour or drive might be, the boy answers, "I can't help its not being all these things you suggested."[118]

Masochism and homosexuality

The active-passive division, as an anthropomorphic conception of sexuality, brings us naturally to the subject of masochism. To be sure, in classical psychoanalysis the status of masochism differs from that of homosexuality: in a chapter entitled "Masochism in Male Homosexuality", Sacha Nacht's book[119] says that "it may seem surprising to couple a perversion with a masochistic neurosis" — surprising, because all psychoanalysis begins with a preliminary bow to the Freudian dictum that "perversion is the negative of neurosis". But we know from experience that whatever the precautions taken by the language of analysis, perversion inevitably assumes the character of a neurosis, from the moment it enters the psychiatrist's explanatory discourse. Thus, for Nacht, the same mechanism leads both to a passive homosexuality and to a moral masochism — the fear of man as the father image, the passive feminine identification with the mother:

> "At first the boy who is inclined towards the inversion has made an effort to resist. . . . However, that first aggressive instinct stifled, it will turn into masochism. . . . This masochistic disposition is strengthened when the subject puts into practice his homosexual inversion."[120]

Here we have another confirmation of the inevitable transformation of the notion of homosexual perversion in its forced Oedipalisation; however contradictory it may appear, the association between masochism and professed inversion (and not between disorders caused by the repression of homosexuality) works well.

113

Inversion is entangled with masochism because perversion is inevitably entangled with neurosis.

So-called "moral" masochism is an Oedipal concentrate; it contains, unadulterated, the sense of guilt which pervades homosexuality. Masochistic Oedipalisation gives sexuality both a clear and a guilty conscience in inversion : pleasure in guilt, the guilt of pleasure and, lastly, the pleasure of guilt, reign supreme. Freud writes in *Three Essays* that clinical analysis of cases of masochistic perversion shows that they are the result of a "primary passive sexual attitude",[121] bound of course to the castration complex, which is formative of the sense of guilt. The analysis of masochism adds one more link to the chain which binds passivity-narcissism-homosexuality-guilt through fear of castration, fear of the outside world and fear of phallus-bearing men and phallus-less women. Thus, according to Sartre, Genêt is playing a game of "loser wins" when he accepts a submissive and consenting humiliation, as someone who allows himself to be sodomised. According to Sartre there is no satisfaction for the person sodomised (for Divine, who goes to masturbate in the toilet after offering himself to his man), because there is no orgasm but the genital one : only shame and pain are anal. The masochist is an invert in terms of pain, enjoying pain as pleasure by reversing the master's imaginary in every detail.

What is interesting here is the process by which psychoanalysis perfects its little juggling act and inevitably strikes down all manifestations of anal erotism with constitutional guilt.

The active-passive categories generally associated with the homosexual, the bugger and the buggered, are correlated with the analytical categories of sadism and masochism. This correlation is made possible by the fact that sadism as defined by Freud permits the establishment of a differentiation, preceding the masculine-feminine one, between active and passive. If we look at this polarity (which appears at the anal stage), "from the point of view of the genital phase. . . . trends with a passive aim are attached to the erotogenic zone of the anal orifice."[122] The transformation of sadism into masochism — sadism turned upon the subject's own self — is part of "the destiny of repression"[123] triggered by the formation of the ego as such; it taints with guilt everything concerned with anal (passive) satisfaction. If maso-

114

chistic pleasure, experienced through the partner's aggression or at the partner's pleasure, is inevitably a guilty pleasure, then according to Freud, that is because it presupposes an "unconscious sense of guilt".[124] This implies that anality, because of the original passive role assigned to it, follows the same destiny as masochism : everything related to the anal is guilty. The buggered person is a masochist, even in spite of himself. He may enjoy himself — but, according to the book, not only has he no right to do so, he *cannot*.

The narcissistic stage is the knot of the differentiation between subject and object, while the anal-erotic stage is the knot of the differentiation between active and passive. Libidinal production enters the Oedipal arena.

The active role of moral masochism in instigating homosexual guilt is made quite clear by Törless's perplexities. At first, Törless is unable to choose between sadism and masochism, not because sadism would be primary and masochism secondary, but because the differentiation requires a vigilant superego whose formation will only take place in the small group itself, through the play of the imaginary among the four students. Törless "pays no attention" to Beineberg's flow of fascistic metaphysics : he cannot situate his desire in relation to a discourse which appears to him to have no direct connection with what is happening. But he will soon understand what it is all about; the sadism which he practises with the other two on Basini stimulates his discovery of the game of shame : "He was ashamed at having delivered up his idea to the others."[125] And Basini's confession, which comes at a time when Törless is wondering with good reason whether he himself is not in turn going to become the masochistic object of his two fellows, puts together the system of the imaginary and of guilt-inducement :

> "He says, if he didn't beat me, he wouldn't be able to help thinking I was a man, and then he couldn't let himself be so soft and affectionate to me."[126]

It is Basini who narrates Reiting's comments to a hesitating Törless, justificatory comments in which Basini himself sees how he is placed : the subdivision of homosexual activity into pleasure and suffering (to beat or be beaten) constructs the pleasure of guilt (the pleasure of pain, the wish to be beaten). It is only through the projection of the imaginary on to the partner that such a system can be constructed. Masochism is no more secondary than sadism is primary. Törless's sadism is more a questioning of sadism, a secondary sadism to his primary masochism. He anxiously questions Basini on his feelings when he is beaten :

> "That's not what I'm after. . . . When I drive all that into you like knives, what goes on in you? . . . Tell me!"[127]

Törless is unable to deal with all the notions which are put to him and whose meaning his desire is ignorant of. His perplexities are those of a polymorphous desire baffled by the signs of the guilt-inducing imaginary. He would like to experience what Basini experiences, but at the same time he feels the disquieting presence of Beineberg's and Reiting's fascinating superegos. He would be Basini, if being Basini did not presuppose the existence of the other two; just as he would be a masochist if that did not imply the existence of sadism, and homosexual if it did not imply the existence of heterosexuality.

The pick-up machine

When Basini stands naked in front of him, Törless experiences a brutal assault of desire, from which he recoils in anguish : "It's a man, damn it!", he whispers to himself. To encounter desire is first of all to forget the difference in the sexes. Similarly Aschenbach comes under the assault of beauty, and he is only able to withstand it by means of a meditation on art : "Aschenbach . . . was astonished anew, yes, startled at the godlike beauty of the young mortal."[128] All metaphors on the miraculous nature of the homosexual encounter boil down to one thing : when desire strikes, there is no room for the imaginary. By comparing the encounter between Jupien and Charlus with the meeting of the bumble-bee and the flower, Proust is able to express the immediate plugging-in which is so alien to the social order; simply entering a drawing-room, on the other hand, represents for the young Proust himself an extreme case of social anxiety, in the form of the imaginary question, "What are they going to think of me?" Hearing the usher roar out his name for the first time at the entrance to the Guermantes' drawing-room, he experiences the unbounded social anxiety of someone who is always afraid that he is the object of a hoax. And is it really by accident that Proust comes immediately after the Duke of Châtellerault, who recognises his lover of the night before in the usher (to whom, of course, he had not then given his real name)?[129] Everything that happens between Charlus and Jupien likewise has no name. Even Tadzio's name is an arbitrary reconstruction on Aschenbach's part. In truth, the pick-up machine is not concerned with names or sexes. The drift where all encounters become possible is the moment in which desire produces and feels no guilt. Anyone who has witnessed the strange balletic quality of a regular homosexual pick-up haunt will be deeply attuned to Proust's description of the innocence of flowers.

It is generally assumed that what we may call homosexual "scattering" — the fact that homosexuals have a multitude of love affairs, each of which may last only a moment — expresses the fundamental instability of the homosexual condition, the search for a dream partner through a series of brief, unsatisfactory affairs. The homosexual pick-up scene may well be experienced in such a way, at least at the level of what "queers" tell each other or what they have found out about themselves. But instead of translating this scattering of love-energy as the inability to find a centre, we could see it as a system in action, the system in which polyvocal desire is plugged in on a non-exclusive basis. Aschenbach's drift around Venice is connected with a guilty sexuality because it is identified with a single object, the principle being "you lose one person and the world becomes empty". The homosexual condition is experienced as unhappy because its mechanical scattering is translated as absence and substitution. We could say that on the contrary homosexual love is immensely superior, precisely because everything is possible at any moment: organs look for each other and plug in, unaware of the law of exclusive disjunction. Homosexual encounters do not take place in the seclusion of a domestic setting but outside, in the open air, in forests and on beaches. The cruising homosexual, on the look-out for anything that might come and plug in to his own desire, is reminiscent of the "voyaging schizophrenic" described in *L'Anti-Oedipe*. If the homosexual pick-up machine, which is

117

infinitely more direct and less guilt-induced than the complex system of "civilised loves" (to use Fourier's phrase), were to take off the Oedipal cloak of morality under which it is forced to hide, we would see that its mechanical scattering corresponds to the mode of existence of desire itself.

6
THE HOMOSEXUAL STRUGGLE

In Germany at the end of the nineteenth century, Hirschfeld created his Scientific Humanitarian Committee, a movement for the defence and justification of homosexuality in the face of social repression. The "Club Arcadie" in France serves approximately the same purpose. However, what I mean by "homosexual struggle" is essentially different: it is no longer a matter of justifying, or vindicating, or even attempting a better integration of homosexuality within society. I shall now be discussing the way in which recent gay movements, linked up with left-wing activism, have changed or overturned the commonly acknowledged relation between desire and politics. Homosexual action, not action in favour of homosexuality: now that the gay movements have opened this crack, what has really changed?

The revolution of desire

Wilhelm Reich described how the restoration of the law on homosexuality in the USSR corresponded with the rise of stalinism:

> "In March 1934, there appeared a law which prohibits and punishes sexual intercourse between men. . . . This law designated sexual intercourse between men as a 'social crime' to be punished, in lighter cases, with imprisonment of from three to five years. . . . Thus homosexuality was again put in the same category as other social crimes: sabotage, banditism, espionage, etc."[180]

(According to Reich, at the time of the Soviet revolution homosexuality had enjoyed a general climate of tolerance, which was expressed in the fact that the *Soviet Encyclopaedia's* definition of it relied on Hirschfeld and Freud.)[181]

119

Repressive actions are generally much more consistent than revolutionary movements. Reich's analysis was based on the contrast between the Soviet Union's revolutionary nature and its inevitable degeneration. In this same sense, revolutionary movements usually find themselves in the position of accusing the "official" communist parties of treason or degeneration. When a spokesman for the French Communist Party can say something such as "Finally, [the authorities] have always in store, like a fire smouldering under the ashes, a little barricade for the eve of the referendum or a few homosexuals for the First of May,"[1] the united front of people seeking social change is shaken to the core. (In connection with homosexuals in particular, this same spokesman talked about the contrast between "the democratic and revolutionary order" and "leftist mayhem.") The repression of desire, whether it be in the name of the higher interests of mankind or in those of the proletariat, is strictly the same in its effects. The first effect of the appearance of the gay movement has been to expose this equivalence.

It is possible that revolutionary politics are in themselves repressive processes. In this case, where does the opposition between Reich and Freud lead to? Reich thought in terms of revolutionary politics — he even practised a sexual politics (this was the first instance of a revolutionary movement discussing sexuality). To the inevitability of the repression of desire, which Freud had affirmed in *Civilisation and its Discontents,* he opposed a project for sexual revolution which tackled the question of happiness head-on. He saw what Freud refused to see : that the famous "reality principle" is not irremovable but rests in fact on the supremacy of the heterosexual family. He even showed how the social system of repression tries to pass off Oedipal repression as unalterable. He analysed the phenomenon of fascism in terms of desire, thereby rejecting the whining attitude to it which is common both to middle-class liberalism and to ossified marxism. However, Reich's sexual revolution can unfortunately be reduced to the idea that what is repressed is man's natural inclination towards woman and vice-versa. He himself wrote :

"According to sex-economic knowledge, homosexuality is, in a vast majority of cases, a result of a very early inhibition

120

of heterosexual love. . . . (1.) Homosexuality among adults is not a social crime, it does no harm to anybody. (2.) It can be reduced only by establishing all necessary prerequisites for a natural love life among the masses. (3.) Until this goal can be achieved, it must be considered a mode of sexual gratification alongside the heterosexual one and should (with the exception of the seduction of adolescents and children) not be punished."[132]

The sexual revolution solves the problem of homosexuality by making it disappear naturally, with a minimum of repression. Elsewhere Reich indulges in numerous jokes about the homosexuality in Hitler's youth camps,[133] speaking about the "development of homosexual tendencies and relationships between boys who had never thought of it before." Simply coupling the word "sexual" with the word "revolution" cannot get rid of the heterosexual norm. We could add : on the contrary. From this point of view, and however reactionary his political position, Freud shows the greater understanding of polymorphously perverse desire.

Something always seems to go wrong somewhere between desire and revolution; we get the same continual wail both from those who want to but can't (the far left) and from those who can but won't (the Communist Party).

We must give up the dream of reconciling the official spokesmen of revolution to the expression of desire. We cannot force desire to identify with a revolution which is already so heavy with the past history of the "workers' movement". Revolutionary demands must be derived from the very movement of desire; it isn't only a new revolutionary model that is needed, but a new questioning of the content traditionally associated with the term "revolution", particularly the notion of the seizure of power.

The gay movement, along with certain other left-wing movements, has been successful in exposing the reactionary implications of waiting for an upheaval to come from some rough, muscle-bound, virile proletariat.[134] Reich's attempt, through the German Communist Party, to reconcile the revolutionary past with the emergence of desire proved to be grossly reactionary with regard to homosexuality. This may, however, be an indica-

121

tion that radical questioning can spring from politically virgin and totally marginal territory. The apolitical nature of the homosexual question, in the sense of its absence from the sphere of traditional revolutionary politics, may also be its good fortune. All the "radical" movements appearing today share with the gay movement the fact that they are devoid of a political past (the women's movement, ecology, etc.) and are marginal in relation to the questions normally put forward on revolutionary platforms.

The question of homosexuality is one of the many which are not asked so long as those concerned do not themselves do so. It is marginal essentially because it is totally alien to the "masses".

A French progressive weekly, *Politique-Hebdo,* once gave an article on FHAR (the Homosexual Front for Revolutionary Action) the headline "Révolutionnaire par la bande".* The implied criticism was on the one hand that the erection is not terribly revolutionary, and on the other hand that the gay movement strikes only at the fringe, at the margins, and not at the centre of the social problematic. Desire is fated not only to manifest itself by erection alone, but also to indicate thereby that the real centre lies on the margin, i.e. that there is no centre at all.

Revolutionary tradition maintains a clear division between the public and the private. The special characteristic of the homosexual intervention is to make what is private — sexuality's shameful little secret — intervene in public, in social organisation. It demonstrates that alongside (and perhaps in opposition to) conscious political investments which are based on the broad social masses united by their interests, there is a system of unconscious or libidinal investments whose repression depends precisely on the capacity of the political system to think of itself as the only possible one. A reactionary libidinal investment may well coexist with a progressive or revolutionary political investment, in the shadow of the wall dividing private from political life. Daniel Guérin pointed out, in connection with the abovementioned remarks from the French Communist Party, that the presence of homosexuals on the May Day demonstration would

---

* The word *bande* as used here is a pun: it means "margin", but it is also a slang term for "erection" [*trans.*].

certainly not be new : what is new is that homosexuals now shout aloud what they are on such occasions. Besides, the Communist Party says it doesn't so much dislike homosexuality as the mixture of styles, the interference of a purely private (and therefore politically meaningless) affair in the sphere of official relations between the classes.

The gay movement is thus not seeking recognition as a new political power on a par with others; its own existence contradicts the system of political thought, because it relates to a different problematic. The bourgeoisie generates the proletarian revolution, but defines the framework within which the struggle takes place; this we could call the framework of civilisation, from whose historical continuity every social force benefits. In this sense, Freud is right to speak of the discontents existing in civilisation, or as we might say, the discontents *of* civilisation. In a discussion on Fourier, René Schérer notes :

> "In this respect, the appearance of the bourgeoisie and the proletariat is a phenomenon which takes place *within civilisation*. The stakes of the struggle could well be, in this case, the appropriation of *civilisation* by either one of the two classes."[135]

From this point of view the gay movement appears basically uncivilised, and it is not without reason that many people see it as the end of reproduction and thus the end of the species itself. There is no point in speculating whether the class war might be replaced by a war of civilisation, which would have the advantage of adding a cultural and sexual dimension to the political and economic struggle. Going to this extent would mean challenging the very concept of civilisation, and we must retreat with Fourier to the notion of a struggle against civilisation understood as the Oedipal succession of generations. Civilisation forms the interpretative grid through which desire becomes cohesive energy. Wildcat movements among workers, actions which take place outside the commonly accepted political frameworks and which make no formal claims, not even for the seizure of power, are part of the disintegration of that coherence. The most honest leftists will cite the desire for a new society as evidence of absence. It is already too much to believe that the "wildcatter" is a future civilised person, as the child is a future adult. The gay movement is a wildcat movement because it is not the signifier of what might become a new form of "social organisation", a new stage of civilised humanity, but a crack in what Fourier calls "the system of the falsity of civilised loves"; it demonstrates that civilisation is the trap into which desire keeps falling.

Why homosexuality?

While on the one hand Freud is more lucid than Reich as regards the component forces of sexuality, on the other hand — and this is what enables him to keep his discovery under control — he sticks to a reactionary thesis by enclosing desire within the privatisation of the family. Deleuze and Guattari write:

> "There is a thesis which Freud values most of all: the libido invests the social field as such only so long as it is desexualised and sublimated."[136]

But the homosexuality of the gay movement invests the social field directly, without passing through sublimation; in fact it desublimates everything it can by putting sex into everything.

But why homosexuality? What is so special about this particular category, this artificial subdivision of desire? Deleuze and Guattari also claim:

> "For instance, no Homosexual Front is possible so long as homosexuality is caught in a relation of exclusive disjunction with heterosexuality, which refers them both to the same castrating Oedipal blueprint, charged with ensuring their differentiation."[137]

What they do not state, though it explains the actual role played by homosexuality, is that the Oedipal system is not only a system of exclusive disjunction but also the system of oppression of one sexual mode, the heterosexual family mode, over all possible other modes. The Oedipal system actually brings the oppressed sexual modes together, even while it is trying to cut them off from the original non-differentiation of desire. General positions of principle are not enough here: it must be clearly stated, as the quotations in this book illustrate, that what nearly always emerges from the homosexual protest is a protest against the

124

whole Oedipal system, and that the gay movement has brought the entirety of men's sexual problems to the surface. The women's movement has begun to find a response from men in this particular form.

On the other hand, it would be absurd to expect that we could reconstitute the polymorphism of desire by making a simple addition of all the forms of Oedipal sexuality, for example by adding homosexuality to heterosexuality. These forms as such are just arbitrary divisions. The very difference between man and woman is in itself already one of the given factors of the Oedipal family system. And the question which the gay movement raises is not so much that of the particular sexual object as that of the functioning mode of sexuality. It is not through the object and its choice that the non-exclusiveness of desire is revealed, but through its very system of functioning. In this respect there is a lot to be said for the so-called "homosexual" system of pick-ups and mechanical scattering (see the section on the "pick-up machine" at the end of the previous chapter), a system which is so obsessed by sexuality that it often stands accused of lacking soul or feeling.

It is therefore quite useless to contrast bisexuality with homosexuality, as a more accomplished system of sexual diversity. It is even ideologically suspect to seek, in the name of the principle that nothing is excluded, to bring strays back to the form of sexuality which is not only characteristic but dominant in our society. Family heterosexuality dominates the whole of civilised sexuality; it is certainly no liberation to have to go through it. There can be no symmetry between what the gay movement advocates on the one hand and the dominant form of sexuality on the other. In other words, if bisexuality is to be viable, or better — why set a limit? — if there is to be an end to the sexual norm, this must come through the concrete disintegrative process which the gay movement has begun. Some women, and they more than anyone know that heterosexuality is no conquest, say they can only believe in a bisexuality which is derived from homosexuality. However approximate the formula may be, it appears sound : what is repressed in homosexuals is not the love of woman as a particular sexual object but the entire subject-object system which constitutes an oppression of desire.

125

Experience in Europe and the USA has shown that the women's movement and the gay movement have coincided. It is as if society could not bear to see in man what it demands to see in women, as if to dominate women and to repress homosexuality were one and the same thing. We shall therefore not accuse the gay movement of failing to relate to women, lest we reintroduce thereby the very guilt which we have worked to dissolve. Deleuze and Guattari point out that the women's movement is perfectly justified in replying to people who accuse these women of expressing their penis envy, "We are not castrated and we don't give a damn."[138] The gay movement likewise replies that its members are not afraid of the castration which their fear of the relationship with women would seem to imply, and that in any case they are indifferent to such notions. The danger for homosexuality, the trap of desire, lies elsewhere, in what we call its guilt-induced perversion.

The homosexual situation which has been created by the gay movement, as opposed to those which have long been established in society, has the inestimable advantage of being located in fact rather than in principle, in the reality of everyday life where the division between the public and the private is abolished. Some left-wing elements may well have been outraged at Jean Genêt's remark: "Perhaps if I had never gone to bed with an Algerian, I would never have approved of the FLN." A left-wing weekly replied, "We would be the last, whatever our opinion of homosexuality, to demand any repression in that sphere. But the matter gets worrying when politics are thrown into it." It all comes back to the French Communist Party's remarks. Kicking over the traces causes a scandal. Live it, but don't mention it in public. Significantly *Minute,*[139] a publication which specialises in anti-Arab racism, also picked on what Genêt said, stating that "In this sphere at least, colonialism is practised in reverse." Between many Arabs and many homosexuals there are desiring relations which are unacceptable; so the cloak of Oedipal moral decency is thrown over them, which may well deeply affect those concerned. In Arab nationalism as expressed by some Arab students in France there is ready talk about "back-to-front colonialism", though this is not something we can joke about: they are talking about colonialist pederasty, which

126

means the exploitation of young Arabs for a modest fee. But they insist on the degenerate and debauched nature of homosexuality as a colonialist invention, and admit its existence among Arabs only as a substitute, when relations with women are difficult. We find the same attitude concerning prisoners, as if homosexuality were a necessity for them — a poor man's sexuality, the sexuality of the oppressed as opposed to middle-class, degenerate homosexuality. We have to admit that a desiring relation of this type can apparently be experienced only if necessity is the excuse. But the guilt-inducing nature of such explanations makes them suspect, and offers the gay movement the chance to make an intervention based not on a kind of solidarity of principle but on a desiring relation.

There is one category among the oppressed which inspires a particular degree of civilised concern : the young, the sexual minors. The Oedipus complex is based on the succession of the generations and on the conflict between child and adult. It is obviously the adult who leads the child astray; if there is a homosexual between the two of them, it is inevitably the adult. Now many young people are affirming their desire to be seduced, their right to dispose of their own sexuality. In the above-mentioned article, *Minute* abandons its jesting tone in order to deal with this serious matter :

> "All this could just be grotesque. But when homosexual schoolboys are invited to organise and to expose their teachers' 'repression', it all becomes loathesome."[140]

The main opposition to psychoanalysis stems from the fact that it speaks about the existence of an infantile sexuality, even though immediately it is discovered it gets fed into the Oedipus complex and sublimation, and imprisoned in the famous "latency period". Here too, as in the case of the Arabs, political thought presupposes the existence of groups of oppressors (adults — or Europeans) and oppressed (children — or Arabs), in order to exclude any possible desiring relation. It then becomes quite easy to say that the relation in question is due to oppression.

The "political" positions of the gay movement can therefore not be derived from the elementary classification into progressive and reactionary, because they challenge this classification.

The relationship between the gay movement and other kinds of struggle for the destruction of the repressive authorities is hardly comparable with the relationships which revolutionary political movements usually have between them. It was for the sake of the struggle against sexism, the cult of masculinity and the American version of war as a kind of "manly game" that the gay movement took part in the struggle against the war in Vietnam. This kind of distinction may seem artificial to civilised political thinking. Nevertheless, it carries some weight of its own. This is how the teeming confusion of youth movements, women's movements, gay movements, ecological movements, community movements etc., experience politics. They all start from a particular desiring situation (their relation to sex, to nature, to the environment) and not, as the traditional workers' movement would like, from a strategy based on general political theories; the political world is founded on the debate between these theories, which are all equally true whatever the bearer. The appearance of "autonomous movements", movements which reject the law of the signifier all the more because they create a law for themselves, has completely upset the political world.

The confusion is total, since the links between these desiring situations do not occur according to the logical model of the signifier-signified but prefer to follow the logic of the event. It is therefore no use trying to work out the relationships between these movements in rational or strategic terms. It is incomprehensible that the gay movement should be closely connected with the ecological movement. Nevertheless, it is so. In terms of desire, the motor car and family heterosexuality are one and the same enemy, however impossible it may be to express this in political logic.

The perverse trap

It is not suitable to employ a triumphant tone when speaking about the social desiring struggle. I have already pointed out how unsatisfactory it is to confuse the term "homosexual" with "homosexual desire". There is always a trap waiting for desire, inscribing the law in the heart of the dispute. We know how acceptable homosexuality is when it is seen as something perverse.

128

A homosexual movement certainly cannot free itself from this perverse integration by simply announcing its presence. The trick of social repression is to forbid it in a loud enough voice to focus desire on what is supposed to be forbidden, so that anyone who wants to ignore the prohibition can have a taste of the transgression. *France-Dimanche* opened its investigation, not with the usual historical reference to the Greeks but, with successful journalistic daring, by introducing FHAR. The title of the first article was, "In France today, homosexuals dare to come out into the open". We can sense the acid taste of transgression in "daring" to come out into "the open". The taste of scandal, the political striptease, contain their own antidote. They wrap the gay movement in an apologetic discourse, they freeze the event into a role.

This is all the more evident when that newspaper's anti-desiring operation, like all great liberal debates, offers the testimony of doctors and homosexuals alongside each other : "We shall open our pages to homosexuals who will describe their own experiences. Doctors who have been studying these problems for years will speak about their work," was the promise. The militants of the gay movement have just as much of a natural tendency to become specialists on homosexuality as psychiatrists and social workers.

Homosexual desire has got entangled in a game of shame, and it is no less perverse to turn this into a game of pride. In fact people are always a little ashamed of being proud of being homosexual. By becoming passionate propagandists of homosexuality, referring not to Freudian bisexuality but to a homosexual "nature" as opposed to the heterosexual one, they remain enclosed within the system of Fourier's "civilised loves".

The pervert is essentially "civilised", which is what Fourier is expressing when he speaks about civilisation as "subversive order". For him, civilisation is subversive because it organises desire in a guilty way. Subversion and perversion are therefore not synonymous with liberation : quite the contrary. Schérer, in his introduction to Fourier, writes : "Civilisation is false because its movement is the thwarted progress of passions, their *subversive rise*." Because it operates "as a theoretical whole which has practically the effect of a repressive totality", what we need in order to break it up is "not so much a *good* theory, but the liberation of the passions whose rise it has hampered".[141] The "subversive rise" of the passions refers not only to their repression but also to their access to the status of perversion.

Civilised perversion, the perverse status of desire, is the worm in the rose of passion. To assume perversity is to accept, in the case of homosexuals, the notion of an opposition between two clearly defined sexes, and to believe that a few men donning femininity is enough to question this opposition. Sartre's conception is that Genêt is a homosexual who *takes pride* in betraying his masculinity and is therefore the bearer of a great significance.[142] But the gay movement does not care to describe itself as the instrument of a betrayal: to betray the law of normality means continuing to recognise its existence. "Queens" in drag are not "feminine" : that is not why they possess such a challenging force. Sartre comes closer to the reality of the movement when he writes, "Genêt's femininity is an evanescent being, a pure challenge to masculinity." "Queens" do not want to be either men or women : they carry the decoding of the fluxes of desire to its limit.

It is not the perverse psychology of homosexuality, its procession of roles and mirrors, that is interesting. The essential effect of the gay movement is first of all its crude sexualisation of the social field; the most common criticism made of it is that it speaks only about sex, and not about love.

Young revolutionaries are all the more keen to revive the humanist values which they believe the bourgeoisie to be constantly betraying even as it mouths them. The "commune" movement, for example, reappropriates the values of "real" interhuman relationships which an inhuman capitalism seeks daily to destroy. However, the attempt to reactivate liberal humanist values usually drowns this movement in gushes of glutinous affectivity, in which the analysis of "psychological" problems ends up by occupying the entire field of relationships. Capitalism decodes the fluxes of desire and immediately circumscribes them within privatisation. It is no use trying to turn the clock back. We can say the same thing about "respect for the human personality" as Marx said about the family in *The Communist Manifesto* : capitalism has effectively destroyed the social substructure of these territorialisations, and they can therefore only reappear in the perverse form of artificial re-territorialisations. This impossible return is expressed among revolutionary youth in the enormous growth of what Deleuze and Guattari call "the abject desire to be loved". The sexualisation of the world heralded by the gay movement pushes capitalist decoding to the limit and corresponds to the dissolution of the human; from this point of view, the gay movement undertakes the necessary dehumanisation.

Against the pyramid

By no means the least of the functions of the gay movement is to confront the confrontation movement itself with the abolition of the difference between public and private, the disintegration of the civilised illusion common to the political world, and the collapse of this civilisation's imaginary affective system. It has discovered forms of oppression even among the forms of struggle. The association of the words "homosexuality" and "revolution" seems to possess a demystifying function which Huey P. Newton once acknowledged in the following terms:

> "Nothing gives us the right to say that a homosexual cannot also be a revolutionary. And no doubt it is only because of prejudice that I say: *even* a homosexual can be revolutionary. On the contrary, it is more than likely that a homosexual will be among the most revolutionary of the revolutionaries."[143]

There is no innocent association between the two words, no chance of a peaceful coexistence between the gay movement and the more traditional forms of politics. The political system operates on the relation between signifier and signified, on the pyramidal relation between representative and masses. The gay movement questions the signified "masses", first of all by showing that the separate division of these masses is itself the product of "civilised ideology". The homosexual problem is marginal, but at the same time it is undoubtedly a mass one, assuming (and one generally does) the universal nature of bisexuality in Freud's sense. However, this mass scale is not translated into

131

the existence of a large social mass delegating representatives. These masses are not organised according to molar system of the large-scale social groupings and their institutions, but according to that of small subject groups. The gay movement's characteristic is that it apparently has no real centralisation (nor any real democracy), no slogans to send round, no representatives. We have already seen (in chapter three) that an annular desiring system would abolish the phallic hierarchy, which finds its concrete expression in the delegation of powers. We have seen that politics is divided between people who want to but can't and people who can but won't. The means of proceeding from desire to power is commonly believed to be the political organisation. In his introduction to Fourier, Schérer points out that the usual case against Fourier is that although he forged a theory, this was insufficient without the addition of an organising practice :

> "Does the revolutionary 'reappropriation' of Fourier mean that it is enough to add to Fourierist 'theory', which has remained inoperative, the 'revolutionary organisation' which would project it into reality?"[144]

This kind of division in itself constitutes the reign of the political, whereas what makes Fourier's thought "so close to initially disorganised masses" is perhaps "the virtue of his very rejection of organisation".

The tempo of politics is the tempo of strategy, of the division between means and aims. In Schérer's words :

> "The pattern — unorganised practice/theory/organised practice/readjustment of the theory of organisation in terms of the practice — has dialectically structured the field of the class war up to the present day. Its tempo is one of phases and pauses. Structurally, it is based on hierarchies and privileges."[145]

The true representative of the masses is the person who is able to distinguish these hierarchies and privileges, and to organise the relation between the signifier and the signified. This tempo can be contrasted with Fourier's naïve injunction to the reader in *Avis aux civilisés relativement à la prochaine métamorphose sociale* to get ready now because the change is coming in six months' time. The gay movement is related to the ungenerating-ungenerated of the orphan desire, and is unaware of the passing of generations as stages on the road to better living. It knows nothing about "sacrifice now for the sake of future generations", that cornerstone of socialist enlightenment.

Deleuze and Guattari write as follows:

> "A revolutionary group remains, as far as the pre-conscious is concerned, a *subjected group,* even when winning power and for as long as that power itself reflects a form of mastery which continues to enslave and crush desiring production. . . . A *subject group,* on the contrary, is one whose libidinal investments are in themselves revolutionary; it introduces desire into the social field."[146]

The gay movement can be the producer of subject groups in this sense. Of course, the subject group has a tendency to be subjected — for example, in the course of affirming its perversity. The group which is composed of individuals, the phallic and hierarchical group, is subjected; it obeys civilised institutions whose values it adopts because the individual feels weaker than the institution, and because the individual's tempo is circumscribed by death while the institutions are apparently immortal. In the subject group, the opposition between the collective and the individual is transcended; the subject group is stronger than death because the institutions appear to it to be mortal. The homosexual subject group — circular and horizontal, annular and with no signifier — knows that civilisation alone is mortal.

133

7
CONCLUSION

The "heteroclite" nature of homosexual desire makes it dangerous to the dominant sexuality. Every day a thousand kinds of
homosexual behaviour challenge the classifications imposed on
them. The unification of the practices of homosexual desire under
the term "homosexuality" is as imaginary as the unification of
the component drives in the ego.

There is a form of repression against homosexual practice
which corresponds in normal sexuality to the fear of emptiness,
of the absence of another person, the limitation which haunts
normal sexuality. Let us recall the explanations which school-
children receive on this subject. Their education is essentially
based on the repression of masturbation; the parents or the
teacher generally explain to the child that reciprocal masturbation, or any other manifestation of homosexual desire, is not so
much blameworthy as useless. It is, they say, an unconscious
form of sexual activity which will one day be naturally directed
towards women. It is hardly even sexuality yet, just pre-sexuality.
You will inevitably get over it : it will disappear spontaneously.
Homosexual practices are considered as a non-sexuality, as something which hasn't found its form, for sexuality is exclusively
heterosexual. Treating these forms of pleasure with contempt
and enforced oblivion is a good way of making them disappear.
Homosexuality is reduced to non-sexuality because real sexuality
is the sexuality of identifiable persons, of the Oedipus complex.
And it is here that the frightening non-humanity of homosexual
desire appears.

The route from homosexual desire to homosexuality starts with
a primary, an-Oedipal homosexuality and finishes with a secondary homosexuality which is neurotic, perverse and Oedipalised.

Deleuze and Guattari demonstrate this contrast using Proust's
writings :

> "Proust . . . contrasts two types of homosexuality, or rather
> two regions of which only one is Oedipal, exclusive and

134

depressive, whereas the other is schizoid, an-Oedipal, enclosed and inclusive."[147]

Proust himself writes:

"Some, those no doubt who have been most timid in childhood, are scarcely concerned with the material kind of the pleasure they receive, provided they can associate it with a masculine face. Whereas others, whose sensuality is doubtless more violent, imperiously give their material pleasure certain definite localisations."[148]

Undoubtedly: the latter are described as able to love women too, and this seems to interest Deleuze and Guattari particularly. We should note here the materialistic nature of the satisfaction taken, its direct reference to the imperative localisation of the component drive. Homosexual desire is perverse in the Freudian sense, i.e. it is simply an-Oedipal, as long as it expresses the disorganisation of the component drives. It becomes neuroticallly perverse in the ordinary sense when it relates to a face, when it enters the sphere of the ego and the imaginary.

Thus what the Oedipal construction manages to eliminate or channel is the sum of the challenges which are made by homosexual desire. Oedipal sexuality is based, as is the entire family universe, upon a game of imaginary oppositions which follow the rule of the double-bind. The double closure of false choices is obvious everywhere. (1) Between the private and the public. We have seen how Oedipal homosexuality is caught in the dialectics of confession, the airing of the dirty little secret. Homosexuality focuses the imaginary game by being both the extremely private (the ultimate personal problem) and the extremely public element of confession. (2) Between merciless jealousy-competition and the illusion of the "human community". We have seen the ambiguities which are concealed by the term "social sense" coupled with the sublimation of homosexuality (see p. 85). (3) Between natural biology and guilt-inducing psychology. We have seen that the "nature" which formed the basis of the legal code is as reactionary as the psychology which lays down the foundations of the ego. (4) Between life and death, the two primary manifestations of civilisation.

The challenge to these false choices made by homosexual desire calls for a different pattern. The gay movement denounces both the idealistic sublimation of the social sense and the merciless confrontation between "individuals". It knocks down the dividing wall between biology and psychology, turning Nature from a guilt-inducing reference to a term of equivalence with the immediacy of desire. It demonstrates that the orphaned Unconscious knows neither death nor life, neither the generation of the ego nor the anxiety of its disappearance. A doctor quoted above (p. 55) undertook to eliminate the unconscious killer lurking in every homosexual. The great fear of homosexuality is translated into a fear that the succession of generations, on which civilisation is based, may stop. Homosexual desire is neither on the side of death nor on the side of life; it is the killer of civilised egos.

Civilisation is the assumption of sex or the repression of it, through the individual/society double-bind. Deleuze and Guattari write:

> "We are heterosexual statistically or in a molar sense, homosexual personally (whether we are aware of it or not), and finally transexual in an elementary or molecular sense."[149]

Grouped homosexual desire transcends the confrontation between the individual and society by which the molar ensures its domination over the molecular. It is the slope towards transexuality through the disappearance of objects and subjects, a slide towards the discovery that in matters of sex everything is simply communication.

NOTES

1. Alfred Adler, *Das Problem der Homosexualität*, Leipzig, 1930.
2. Havelock Ellis, *Sexual Inversion*, London, 1897 (revised edition, 1923).
3. Kinsey, Pomeroy and Martin, *Sexual Behaviour in the Human Male*, London, 1948, p. 656.
4. *Ibid.*, p. 639.
5. Jean-Paul Sartre, *Saint-Genêt, Actor and Martyr*, London, 1964.
6. Freud, "Psychoanalytic Notes on an Autobiographical Account of a Case of Paranoia", in *The Complete Psychological Works of Sigmund Freud*, vol. 12, p. 59.
7. *Ibid.*, p. 59.
8. *Ibid.*, p. 43.
9. *Ibid.*, p. 43.
10. Sandor Ferenczi, "On the Part Played by Homosexuality in the Pathogenesis of Paranoia", in *First Contributions to Psychoanalysis*, London, 1952, pp. 156-7.
11. *Ibid.*, p. 170.
12. *Ibid.*, p. 175.
13. *Ibid.*, p. 175.
14. Ferenczi, "The Nosolgy of Male Homosexuality (Homo-Erotism)", in *op. cit.*, pp. 296-7.
15. *Ibid.*, p. 296.
16. Freud, "Psychoanalytic Notes" etc., in *op. cit.*, vol. 12, p. 62.
17. *Ibid.*, p. 61.
18. Freud, "Some Neurotic Mechanisms in Jealousy, Paranoia and Homosexuality", in *op. cit.*, vol. 18, p. 232.
19. W. H. Gillespie, "Homosexualité", in *Revue française de psych-analyse*, July/August, 1965. Translated from French.
20. *Revue de la gendarmerie belge*, no. 38, Brussells, 1969.
21. Havelock Ellis, *op. cit.*
22. Gustave Macé, *La police parisienne : mes lundis en prison*, Paris, 1889.
23. Wilhelm Stekel, *Impotence in the Male*, London, 1940, vol. 1, p. 265.
24. Alexis Lykiard (trans.), *Lautréamont's Maldoror*, London, 1970.
25. *Le Monde*, Paris, 24 July 1961.
26. Quoted by Dr Escoffier Lambiotte in *Le Monde*, 5 July 1972.
27. D. J. West, *Homosexuality*, London, 1955.
28. Hans Giese, *L'homosexualité de l'homme*, Paris, 1968.
29. Georges Henyer, *Les troubles mentaux*, Paris, 1968.
30. Freud, "An Autobiographical Study", in *op. cit.*, vol. 20, p. 38.
31. Freud, "Three Essays on Sexuality", in *op. cit.*, vol. 7, p. 145.
32. *Ibid.*
33. W. H. Gillespie, *op. cit.* Translated from French.

34. *Ibid.*
35. *Ibid.*
36. Freud, "On Narcissism: an Introduction", in *op. cit.*, vol. 14, p. 78.
37. Wilhelm Stekel, *op. cit.*, p. 261.
38. Sacha Nacht, *Le masochisme*, Paris, 1948.
39. Freud, "On Narcissism'" etc., in *op. cit.*, vol. 14, p. 88.
40. *Ibid.*, p. 102.
41. *Ibid.*, p. 101.
42. *Revue française de psychanalyse*, July/August, 1965.
43. Alfred Adler, *op. cit.*
44. C. Duffy, *Sex and Crime*, New York, 1965.
45. Solyom and Miller, *Behaviour Research*, 1965.
46. Deleuze and Guattari, *L'Anti-Oedipe, Capitalisme et schizophrénie*, Paris, 1972.
47. Proust, *Sodom and Gomorrah* (translated by C. Scott Moncrieff as *Cities of the Plain*), New York, 1927.
48. *Ibid.*, p. 21.
49. Jean-Paul Sartre, *op. cit.*
50. Proust, *Contre Sainte-Beuve*, Paris, 1954.
51. Proust, *Sodom and Gomorrah*, p. 23-4.
52. Louis Canler, *Autobiography of a French Detective*, London, 1864.
53. Proust, *Sodom and Gomorrah*, p. 31.
54. Proust, *Contre Sainte-Beuve*, p. 124.
55. Proust, *Sodom and Gomorrah*, p. 3.
56. *Ibid.*, p. 4.
57. *Ibid.*, p. 6.
58. *Ibid.*, p. 7.
59. *Ibid.*, p. 45.
60. Deleuze and Guattari, *op. cit.*
61. *Ibid.*
62. Sandor Ferenczi, "The Nosology of Male Homosexuality" etc., in *op. cit.*, p. 317.
63. Ferenczi, "Stimulation of the Anal Erotogenic Zone as a Precipitating Factor in Paranoia", in *Final Contributions to Psychoanalysis*, London, 1955, p. 297.
64. *Ibid.*, p. 298.
65. Albert Moll, *L'inversion sexuelle*, 1891.
66. Georges Darien, *Le voleur*, Paris, 1898.
67. Ralph R. Greenson, "Homosexualité et identité sexuelle", in *Revue française de psychanalyse*, July/August, 1965. Translated from French.
68. *Ibid.*
69. *Ibid.*
70. *Ibid.*
71. Thomas Mann, *Death in Venice*, translated by H. T. Lowe-Porter, London, 1955, p. 63.
72. *Ibid.*, p. 76.

73. Freud, "Some Neurotic Mechanisms" etc., in *op. cit.*, vol. 18, p. 223.
74. *Ibid.*, p. 224.
75. *Ibid.*, p. 225.
76. *Ibid.*, p. 225.
77. *Ibid.*, p. 226.
78. *Ibid.*, p. 232.
79. *Ibid.*, p. 232.
80. Freud, "Family Romances", in *op. cit.*, vol. 9, p. 237.
81. *Ibid.*, p. 237.
82. *Ibid.*, p. 237.
83. Deleuze and Guattari, *op. cit.*
84. Gustave Macé, *op. cit.*
85. See Freud, *Totem and Taboo.*
86. Alfred Adler, *op. cit.*
87. Freud, "Some Neurotic Mechanisms" etc., in *op. cit.*, vol. 18, p. 232.
88. *Ibid.*, p. 232.
89. Jacques Corrazé, *Les dimensions de l'homosexualité.*
90. Devereux, "Considérations ethno-psychanalytiques sur la notion de parenté", in *L'homme,* July, 1965.
91. Deleuze and Guattari, *op. cit.*
92. Freud, "Three Essays on the Theory of Sexuality", in *op. cit.*, vol. 7, p. 187.
93. *Ibid.*
94. Jean-Paul Sartre, *op. cit.*
95. Freud, "Three Essays" etc., in *op. cit.*, vol. 7.
96. *Ibid.*, p. 148.
97. *Ibid.*, p. 162-3.
98. *Ibid.*, pp. 136-60.
99. *Ibid.*, p. 205.
100. *Ibid.*, p. 149.
101. Proust, *Sodom and Gomorrah,* p. 21.
102. Freud, *Introductory Lectures on Psychoanalysis,* London, 1922, p. 256.
103. Sandor Ferenczi, "The Nosology of Male Homosexuality" etc., in *First Contribution to Psychoanalysis,* pp. 298-9.
104. Freud, "Three Essays" etc., in *op. cit.*, vol. 7, p. 146.
105. Sandor Ferenczi, "The Nosology of Male Homosexuality" etc., in *op. cit.*, pp. 299-300.
106. *Ibid.*, p. 300.
107. See Freud, "Three Essays" etc., in *op. cit.*, vol. 7, p. 142.
108. Sandor Ferenczi, "The Nosology of Male Homosexuality" etc., in *op. cit.*, p. 302.
109. Jean-Paul Sartre, *op. cit.*, p. 596.
110. Sandor Ferenczi, "The Nosology of Male Homosexuality" etc., in *op. cit.*, p. 300.
111. *Ibid.*, p. 309.

112. See Freud, "Three Essays" etc., in *op. cit.*, vol. 7, p. 136.
113. Sandor Ferenczi, "The Nosology of Male Homosexuality" etc., in *op. cit.*, pp. 301-2.
114. *Ibid.*, p. 302.
115. *Ibid.*, p. 306.
116. *Ibid.*, p. 309.
117. Robert Musil, *Young Törless,* translated by Eithne Wilkins and Ernst Kaiser, London, 1971, p. 147.
118. *Ibid.*, p. 184.
119. Sacha Nacht, *op. cit.*
120. *Ibid.*
121. Freud, "Three Essays" etc., in *op. cit.*, p. 158.
122. Freud, *Introductory Lectures,* p. 370.
123. See Freud, "Instincts and their Vicissitudes", in *The Complete Psychological Works of Sigmund Freud,* vol. 14.
124. See Freud, "The Economic Problem of Masochism", in *op. cit.*, vol. 19.
125. Robert Musil, *op. cit.*, p. 115.
126. *Ibid.*, p. 135.
127. *Ibid.*, p. 137.
128. Thomas Mann, *op. cit.*, p. 66.
129. Proust, *Sodom and Gomorrah,* p. 51.
130. Wilhelm Reich, *The Sexual Revolution,* New York, 1969, p. 209.
131. See P. Hahn, *Français encore un effort.*
132. Wilhelm Reich, *op. cit.*, p. 211.
133. See Reich, *The Mass Psychology of Fascism.*
134 See Front Homosexuel d'Action Révolutionnaire, *Rapport contre la normalité,* Paris 1971.
135. René Schérer, *L'ordre subversif,* Paris, 1972.
136. Deleuze and Guattari, *op. cit.*
137. *Ibid.*
138. *Ibid.*
139. *Minute,* 19 May 1971.
140. *Ibid.*
141. René Schérer, *op. cit.*
142. Jean-Paul Sartre, *op. cit.*, p. 595.
143. Huey P. Newton, "On the Just Struggle of Homosexuals and Women".
144. René Schérer, *op. cit.*
145. *Ibid.*
146. Deleuze and Guattari, *op. cit.*
147. *Ibid.*
148. Proust, *Sodom and Gomorrah,* p. 31.
149. Deleuze and Guattari, *op. cit.*

INDEX

141

142